"Snow's decision to gather into a single boo
poems Rilke composed between 1909 and 1926 but never included
in any of his books is itself an important critical act . . . and enables
us to see the range and uninterrupted fluency of Rilke's productivity
. . . I suspect it is because he has already translated *The Book of
Images*, as well as the two volumes of Rilke's 1907 and 1908 *New
Poems*, that Snow is particularly adept at capturing what one might
call the non-Orphic side of Rilke's voice. Even in the most complex
or rhetorically charged pieces, however, Snow is careful never to
simplify Rilke or to elide the moments of deeply unsettling strange-
ness in his writing. Most important of all, these translations . . .
should finally let us get beyond the simplifications of the Rilke
legend with its cycles of transcendent inspiration and imaginative
paralysis. By now, such a demystification is an essential first step
toward a more genuinely responsive—and responsible—reading of
the poetry itself."

—MICHAEL ANDRÉ BERNSTEIN, *The New Republic*

"These poems have never been done so beautifully in English: for
readers without German, they will be great discoveries; for those
who have known some of them previously, they will deepen their
resonance. This is a splendid achievement."

—JOHN HOLLANDER

"It is wonderful to have a whole new (and sizable) volume of Rilke
poems given us by Edward Snow, who is far and away Rilke's best
contemporary translator—one who never imposes his own per-
sonality or idiosyncrasies of style between us and the original, but
gives to it that respect which proves him worthy of the task."

—DENISE LEVERTOV

"For too long now a sentimental, soft-focus Rilke—Auden's 'Santa
Claus of loneliness'—has prevailed in America. Edward Snow's
Rilke, especially in these austere and unsettling poems, is a different
poet altogether. Snow's intelligence and tact are palpable along the
pulse of every line."   —CHRISTOPHER BENFEY

Also by Edward Snow

PROSE

A Study of Vermeer

TRANSLATIONS

Rainer Maria Rilke: New Poems [1907]

Rainer Maria Rilke: New Poems [1908]: The Other Part

Rainer Maria Rilke: The Book of Images

UNCOLLECTED POEMS

Uncollected Poems

Rainer Maria Rilke

SELECTED AND TRANSLATED

BY *Edward Snow*

BILINGUAL EDITION

North Point Press

Farrar, Straus and Giroux

New York

North Point Press
A division of Farrar, Straus and Giroux
19 Union Square West
New York 10003

Translation copyright © 1996 by Edward Snow
All rights reserved
Published in Canada by HarperCollinsCanadaLtd
Printed in the United States of America
First published in 1996 by North Point Press
First North Point paperback edition, 1997

The Library of Congress has catalogued the hardcover edition as follows:
Rilke, Rainer Maria, 1875–1926.
[Poems. English. Selections]
Uncollected poems / Rainer Maria Rilke ; translated from the
    German by Edward Snow. — 1st ed.
        p.   cm.
    Includes index.
        I. Snow, Edward A.   II. Title.
PT2635.I65A267   1995
831'.912—dc20   94-24438
                                                      CIP

Contents

Introduction   ix

Forget, forget   3
You don't know nights of love?   5
Sharp castle-break   7
Moonlit Night   9
Judith's Return   11
To Lou Andreas-Salomé   13
Pearls roll away   17
Ah, as we prayed for human help   19
O the curves of my longing through the cosmos   21
Come when you should   23
I, knower   27
The almond trees in bloom   29
The Spanish Trilogy   31
The Raising of Lazarus   37
The Spirit Ariel   41
Straining so hard against the strength of night   45
We don't know what we spend   49
Long you must suffer   51
The hawthorn   53
Unknowing before the heavens of my life   55
Overflowing heavens of squandered stars   57
Narcissus [I]   59
Narcissus [II]   61
Christ's Descent into Hell   65
Now we wake up with our memory   67
Thinking you   69
Assault me, music, with rhythmic fury!   71

Behind the innocent trees 73
Head of Amenophis IV in Berlin 75
The way that bright planet, the moon 77
Tears, tears that break out of me 79
Once I took you face into / my hands 81
The Great Night 83
Looking up from my book 85
You the beloved / lost in advance 87
See the carefree insect 89
Turning 91
Lament 95
"One Must Die Because One Has Known Them" 97
Almost as on the last day 99
To Hölderlin 101
On the mountains of the heart cast out to die 105
Again and again 107
Ah misery, my mother tears me down 109
The Death of Moses 111
Death 113
The Words of the Lord to John on Patmos 115
The body's crossroads 121
Now the stag becomes part of earth 123
Gray love-snakes 125
The transformed speaks only to relinquishers 127
To Music 129
God won't be lived like some light morning 131
The Doll. Temptation! 133
To have come through it 135
The Hand 137
As long as you catch self-thrown things 139
. . . When will, when will, when will it be enough 141
Antistrophes 143

We, in the grappling nights   147
My shy moonshadow   149
Vase Painting   151
Odette R. . . .   153
Imaginary Career   155
Lachrymatory   157
We're only mouth   159
Heart's swing   161
Play the deaths swiftly through   165
For Max Picard   167
That we lose nothing   169
For Hans Carossa   171
The Magician   173
Will-o'-the-Wisps   175
As once the winged energy of delight   177
Early Spring   179
Transience   181
A Walk   183
Do you still remember   185
Wild Rosebush   187
By the sun-accustomed street   189
What birds plunge through   191
Unsteady scales of life   193
World was in the face of the beloved   195
Ah, adrift in the air   197
A furrow in my brain   199
Palm of the Hand   201
Night. Oh you face against my face   203
Gravity   205
Mausoleum   207
Somewhere the flower of farewell blooms   209
More unconcealed the land   211

Autumn   213

O bright gleam of a shy mirror image!   215

. . . When from the merchant's hand   217

Ah, not to be cut off   219

Undeterrable   221

Now it is time that gods   223

Rose, O pure contradiction   225

Gong [I]   227

Idol   229

Gong [II]   231

But if you'd try this   233

Earlier, how often, we'd remain   235

The birdcalls begin their praise   237

Brother body is poor   239

Garden, by approaching rains   241

Elegy   243

Full Power   247

Arrival   249

Come, you last thing   251

Notes   255

Index of titles and first lines in German   259

Index of titles and first lines in English   263

Introduction

After Rilke completed the second part of the *New Poems* in 1908, he virtually ceased publishing volumes of poetry. *Requiem* (occasioned by the death of Paula Becker) appeared in 1909, the poem cycle *The Life of the Virgin Mary* in 1913, but nothing major until the sudden appearance in 1923 of the *Duino Elegies* and the *Sonnets to Orpheus*—and then nothing further from the time of their publication until Rilke's death from acute leukemia in December 1926.

The story we tell of these circumstances (largely at the prompting of Rilke's own letters) goes something like this: After more than a decade of free, uninterrupted productivity, Rilke was gradually drawn by his work on *The Notebooks of Malte Laurids Brigge* into a realm of conflict and self-doubt—to such a degree that after that prose work's publication in 1910 he found himself directionless and existentially exhausted, a beginner unable to begin, feeling more and more estranged from the "task" of poetry and yet looking to it increasingly for some definitive, life-answering statement. The years from 1910 through 1922 thus become Rilke's "crisis" years, the crisis deepened by his failure to sustain work on the *Elegies* begun at Duino in 1912, and not resolved until the whirlwind completion of those poems at Muzot in February 1922, accompanied by the virtually unwilled "dictation" of the *Sonnets to Orpheus*, the latter a kind of gift or bonus confirming the high oracular achievement of the *Elegies* and taking its own place as Rilke's one great "post-crisis" work.

So powerfully does this narrative influence our conception of the later Rilke that it can come as something of a shock to learn that the poet, both during his crisis years and after them, was writing poems continuously, often prolifically—in letters, in guest books, in presentation copies, and above all in the pocket-books he always carried with him. Both the quantity and the variety of this uncollected poetry[1] are astonishing. There are over five hundred pieces,

---

1. By the uncollected poetry I mean, following Leishman (below), all the German poems not collected and published in book form by Rilke himself. Rilke did from time to time allow individual "uncollected" poems to be published in the *Insel-Almanach* and other periodicals.

ranging from completed poems of great fluency and poise, to head-long statements that hurtle through their subjects, to brief, un-assuming epiphanies that traverse consciousness like fireflies, to fragments that vary from hard aphoristic kernels ("The transformed speaks only to relinquishers. All / holders-on are stranglers"), to brief forays into the subconscious ("The Doll. *Temptation!* / The loaded doll, which falls into the chasm"), to self-contained, visionary excerpts (". . . When from the merchant's hand / the balance passes over / to the angel, who in the heavens / stills and soothes it with space's equanimity . . ."). It is a formidable body of work. For all its miscellany, there is the sense of an alternate aesthetic informing it, easing distinctions between finishedness and non-finishedness and allowing poetry to take shape with minimal concern for openings and roundings off.

Surprise deepens as one encounters one superb poem after an-other in this assemblage—not just obvious masterpieces such as "The Spirit Ariel" and "The Death of Moses," but a host of small, unprepossessing stunners like "Early Spring":

Harshness disappeared. Suddenly caring spreads itself
on the field's uncovered gray.
Small rivulets change their intonations.
Tendernesses, inexpertly,

reach toward the earth from space.
Roads run far into the land, foretelling it.
Unexpectedly you see its rising's
visage in the empty tree.

After enough such beautifully pitched poems, one has to wonder what accounts for this body of work's neglect—by Rilke himself and in Rilke criticism and biography up to the present day.

Explanations range from the mundane to the obscure. The poems themselves were assembled only gradually after Rilke's death, in awkward stages (the pocket-books were not made available until 1945, and those from entire years may be lost), and J. B. Leishman's rushed translation of the entire corpus, for all the bravery of the undertaking, has served in its near-unreadability as a kind of death's-head keeping English-speaking readers away.[2] More subtly estranging is the German edition's division of the work into separate sections it designates "completed works" (*Vollendetes*), "dedications" (*Widmungen*), and "drafts" (*Entwürfe*)—an arrangement that makes it impossible to experience the poems in their temporal succession, and imposes on them the very distinctions they so curiously blur.[3]

Beyond such problems of access and presentation, however, there is the ever-present myth of Rilke's *Duino* crisis, and that myth's way of obscuring whatever might contradict it or undermine its drama. Rilke's own neglect of the uncollected poems seems to stem from this phenomenon. Consider his complaint in a letter of 1915 to Princess Marie, his host and benefactor at Duino: "For five years now, ever since *Malte Laurids* closed behind me, I've been standing around as a beginner, though as a beginner who can't begin."[4] Rilke must have truly felt this blockage, since he expressed it so often in his letters. But viewed in the light of the uncollected poems composed during the years he mentions, it is sheer mythologizing. Immediately after *Malte Laurids* there is not stagnation but modest growth. And then in 1913 and 1914—hard on the heels of the first suspension of the *Duino* project—there is an explosion of creative brilliance. Rilke composed more than 150 poems during these two years, many of them among the greatest he ever wrote: "The Spanish Trilogy," "The Raising of Lazarus," "The Spirit Ariel," "Christ's Descent into Hell," "Once I took your face into / my hands," "The Great Night," "Turning," " 'One Must Die Because One Has Known Them,' " "To Hölderlin," "Again and again," "On the mountains of the heart cast out to die"—to cite only the best known. Evidently Rilke, once he had become obsessed with the project of the *Duino Elegies*, could not accept these poems as validations. There

2. Rainer Maria Rilke, *Poems 1906 to 1926*, trans. J. B. Leishman (Norfolk: New Directions, 1957). Leishman gives a concise summary of the poems' bibliographic history in the opening pages of his long introduction to this volume.

3. Rainer Maria Rilke, *Sämtliche Werke*, ed. Ruth Sieber Rilke and Ernst Zinn, 6 vols. (Frankfurt: Insel, 1955–66), vols. 2 and 6.

4. Quoted and translated by Michael Hamburger, *An Unofficial Rilke* (London: Anvil Press Poetry, 1981), p. 17.

is no indication that he ever considered publishing them together in a volume,[5] and the self-fashioning aspect of his consciousness seems to have all but erased them. But they are major accomplishments nevertheless, and one would expect even the briefest treatment of Rilke's poetic career to spotlight the period between late 1912 and early 1915 as one of its great florescences. Instead, the work from these years is typically placed within the sad aftermath of the *Elegies'* initial waning ("The avalanche of poetry subsided and, instead of the 'dictated' flow and compulsive utterance, scraps of material had to be laboriously quarried"[6]), or treated as "crisis poems" (especially crisis poems *about* being blocked), or assimilated in some other way to the *Duino* mythos: "It might therefore be said that much of the poetry [Rilke] wrote between 1912 and 1914 is about the price he would have to pay in order to be able to complete the *Duino Elegies*, in order to achieve what might be called the 'angelic vision,' in order to be and remain the only kind of poet he now cared to be."[7]

But there was obviously another kind of poet Rilke cared very much to be: the fact that he kept writing in the manner of the uncollected poems testifies to that. For one of the striking things about those poems is their *difference* from the high vatic mode of the *Duino Elegies* and the *Sonnets to Orpheus*. The two bodies of work seem to stand over against each other, in necessary counterpoise. Against the oracular utterance of the *Elegies*—still sometimes thought of as Rilke's only voice—the uncollected poems articulate a realm of pure occasion: the flooding or flaring of an emotion or a memory, the flash of an idea, the urgency of something willed or wanted or held in wait, acts of attention triggered by or issuing in surprise, upsurges of bitterness or revulsion—even, as in the fol-

5. On three different occasions Rilke did make unpublished selections from the uncollected work. During the war he put together a small collection for Rudolf Kassner entitled *Poems to Night*. In 1922 he and his publisher Anton Kippenberg assembled a group of poems for a proposed appendix to the *Duino Elegies*—an idea that was subsequently discarded. Shortly before his death, he transcribed in a leather-bound volume a set of poems and prose pieces, *From Pocket-Books and Writing Pads (Aus Taschenbüchern und Merkblättern)*, which he sent to Katharina Kippenberg for occasional publication in the *Insel-Almanach*.

6. Siegfried Mandel, *Rainer Maria Rilke: The Poetic Instinct* (Carbondale and Edwardsville: Southern Illinois University Press, 1965), p. 102.

7. Leishman, *Poems 1906 to 1926*, p. 23.

lowing quatrain, moments of tough-minded scorn for the gentler self:

God won't be lived like some light morning.
Whoever climbs down the shaft must give up
earth's repleteness for the craft of mining:
stand hunched and pry him loose in tunnels.

Such poems tend to be fast, headlong, in transit. They touch down at full throttle. Often they appear to compose themselves before one's eyes. An initial impulse, rather than undergoing "development," seems to play itself through, without premeditation, often elliptically and toward no predestined end. Consider the following untitled poem (or "draft"), written the same year as the first *Duino Elegy:*

O the curves of my longing through the cosmos,
and on all the streaks: my being's
flung-outness. Many an aspect returning
only after a thousand years on the sad ellipsis
of its momentum and passing on.
Hastening through the once-existent future,
knowing itself in the year's seasons
or airily, as an exact influence
almost starlike in the overwakeful
apparatus for a short time trembling

Here especially there is an eerie sense of closeness to the poem in process. The first line flings itself out lavishly (one is reminded of some of the great opening lines of Donne's *Holy Sonnets*), and what follows seems to ride that first surge, as it devolves in self-propagating metaphors toward the single, short-lived, unpunctuated light-point, "trembling." It is an eloquent, beautifully paced poem, but it follows its own obscure trajectory, and what it "says" remains suspended in images that images beget, only half translated into some understanding *behind* the poem.

The uncollected poems could thus be said to give us the opposite of "angelic vision." For the most part they aren't interested in consolidating a transcendental consciousness, especially one with visionary wisdom or ex cathedra powers of speech.[8] Everything in them tends to be registered at ground level (which makes all the more remarkable their vivid feeling for the self's sidereal existence, the proliferation in them of arcs, trajectories, bridge systems through space), and some of their most memorable imagery is of dispersal and lavish, even wasteful expenditure. Even a fragment that promises visionary arrival does so in terms that seem calculated to undo the sober questing of the *Elegies:* "Play the deaths swiftly through, the single ones, and you will see— / how it rounds in upon itself, the infinite stream of stars[.]"

There *are* intrusions of second-level consciousness in the poems, but the experience—far from orphic—is usually of a descriptive voice interrupting itself, surprised, as the evoked moment speeds on:

Do you still remember: falling stars, how
they leapt slantwise through the sky
like horses over suddenly held-out hurdles
of our wishes—had we so many?—
for stars, innumerable, leapt everywhere;
almost every look upward was wedded
to the swift hazard of their play,
and the heart felt itself a single thing
beneath that vast disintegration of their brilliance—
and was whole, as though it would survive them!

So much contributes to this poem's complex epiphany: again the ex nihilo opening, the single trajectory, the poem playing itself through; the long-ago other still present in conversation; the heart-catching, throwaway trope, sweeping through three enjambed lines and then caught up in thought before even one's astonishment can

---

8. There are, of course, exceptions, such as the programmatic "What birds plunge through," "As once the winged energy of delight," and "A furrow in my brain"—though even in these poems the oracular advice voices sphinx-like conundrums.

register; a universe where swiftness, chance, and play reign, with the "suddenness" thrust into it by the human game of wishes a strangely integral component; memory not thinking back but confirming the moment's life in consciousness; the elation over something "then" felt "now," and the poem in fact producing that elation; cosmic disintegration as something lavished on the transient human self, *bestowing* the feeling of survival; the subjunctive which frames that feeling somehow not qualifying or undermining it but allowing exclamation.

Rilke wrote "Do you still remember" in 1924 ("Early Spring" belongs to the same year), in the midst of another great creative surge that is all but passed over in the canonical story of his later years. So much narrative force tends to get invested in the climactic, crisis-resolving "dictation" of the remaining *Elegies* and both parts of the *Sonnets to Orpheus* over a three-week span in February 1922 at Muzot (it *does* seem a miraculous achievement) that Rilke's fate seems to close: there seems no *reason* why any poetry should intervene between this consummation and his death in 1926. But in this gap the uncollected work proliferates: some thirty poems in the latter months of 1923, and then, amazingly, more than a hundred in 1924, scarcely any of them negligible and many among Rilke's best: altogether a body of more than two hundred last poems, stretching from the completion of the Orpheus sonnets to the last pocket-book's final entry, a fiercely apocalyptic poem Rilke wrote only weeks before his death.[9]

It seems important to call attention to these last poems, if for no other reason than to stress the fact of their existence. But it would be misleading to regard them as a separate group, given the degree to which they *continue* the mode of the uncollected poems, virtually unaffected by the spectacular orphic interruptions of early 1922. If

9. The profusion of German poems scarcely indicates just how prolific Rilke was in 1924—the very year when the severity of his illness became unmistakable, and his transit between the castle-haven at Muzot and the nearby sanatorium at Valmont began. That year, in addition to the German poems, he composed *Vergers* and *Quatrains Valisans*, French poem sequences of fifty-nine and thirty-six poems respectively. He also entered into the two-year verse correspondence with Erica Mitterer that elicited some forty poems from him between June and August of 1924.

anything, they seem to intensify, distill, define more sharply the character of the uncollected work. But the poems of 1923 and 1924 do seem to enter a new zone, or at least take on a new coloration. Language lightens, yet grows dense with neologism, ellipsis, and wordplay. The change in feeling is elusive; Leishman, attempting to describe it, has recourse to the late Beethoven: "There is an *Umschlag*, a turn, a peripeteia: the prevailing mood is no longer one of strain and tension and effort, but of acceptance, or—to use Rilke's favourite word—of *consentment:* now almost ecstatically joyful, now gravely tranquil, now sadly resigned; often, as in the last music of Beethoven, so much all of these together than [sic] one cannot say which prevails."[10] An even apter analogue might be Klee's last paintings, which, like Rilke's poems, are content to stay small, and which also proliferate, the apparent ease and *slightness* of the thing producing, again as with Rilke, disproportionately intense effects. (Klee's angels, so alien to those of the *Elegies*, would be uncannily at home in the world of the uncollected poems.) Consider "Wild Rosebush," the kind of poem that Rilke seemed able to write at will in 1924:

How it stands out against the darkenings
of the rainy evening, young and pure,
in its tendrils arched everywhere in givingness
and yet absorbed in its rose-being;

the shallow flowers, here and there already open,
each one unasked-for and untended:
thus, immeasurably exceeded by itself
and indescribably self-aroused,

it calls to the wanderer, who in evening
meditation comes past along the road:
Oh look at me, see, over here, how safe I am
and unprotected and having all I need.

10. Leishman, *Poems 1906 to 1926*, p. 37.

This deceptively simple poem is all contradiction, opposition, counterpoise. The isolated rosebush is heightened by its background and yet stands there *against* it, perhaps vulnerably *near* it both in space and in time (the *Verdunkelungen* at work behind the rosebush can suggest not just "darkenings" but deepenings, blackings-out, suppressions, obscure inflictings of harm). The rosebush itself is pure contradiction, a confluence of opposed motives pushed to their extremes: both "absorbed" (*versunken* can range from "sunk" to "immersed" to "engrossed") in its rose-being—and thus both like and unlike the human being who walks past deep in thought—and extravagantly arched out in gestures of self-offering (*ausgeschwungen*, a Rilkean coinage suggesting not only the outward curve of the tendril but the motive force that extends it and perhaps even the desire that signals through it): gestures, it would seem, that go unheeded. The "shallowness" of the open flowers counteracts the bush's "sunkenness" in its rose-being, and contradictory senses of abandonment (achingly forsaken or blissfully outside need) grow almost explicit in the paired participial adjectives (*ungewollt und ungepflegt*): either "unpremeditated and uncultivated"—hence spontaneously wild—or "unwanted and uncared-for," as with an orphan.

As all this descriptiveness builds up in arcane formulations of self-exceeding and self-excitement (do they appear as summings-up or as non sequiturs?), the poem crosses over unexpectedly into the realm of voicing. As it does so—producing another quietly intense epiphany—new oppositions configure. Within the rose-bush's articulation of itself, are not "safe" and "unprotected" in blatant opposition? Or does it only seem so from one's human standpoint? And if the rosebush is set apart from us in the unconflictedness of its contradictions, why the calling out so fervently to the human passerby, the intense desire to make itself seen and heard? Does it wish to offer itself up as an exemplum (as in "See how it might be for you"), or does it long for some connection? Either way, there is a pull. The rosebush and the solitary wanderer are themselves in counterpoise: the one possessing speech but sunk in silent thought, the other mute but calling fervently; the one passing by oblivious, the other straining from its rooted place; both of them solitary against the background "darkenings." And if it is in the nature of things that the wanderer *not* hear the wild rosebush's call, how then account for the poem's own urgently imagined voicing of it? What *human* split does this configure? And last: as the poem rounds to its climax, how is it that the rapture in the voice prevails over its lostness on the human passerby?

The counterpositioning that makes "Wild Rosebush" so rich weaves through the whole of the uncollected poems; it is an obsessive leitmotif. *Gegenüber* is the key German term, whose slight distinctions Rilke seems always to mobilize: opposite, vis-à-vis, over against, facing, compared with, in relation to. Divides become the space of both severance and relation, longing and equipoise; opposites seek (sometimes mutually, sometimes one-sidedly) to bridge, cross over, bind, balance, renew, even stretch taut their "betweenness." Male is posed against female, the face against the universe or the vast night sky. Women renew their tension with their mirror images, Narcissus views his lying lifeless on the water's floor. Cups penetrate each other without clinking, the interval between them remains unchanged. Signals from the other side fail to reach us, change us anyway. The gods learned quickly to simulate halves, while wholeness may have been our worst mistake. "Brother body" must be humored in his sickness by his friend and fellow recluse "consciousness," who is already a peculiar "we." From over there in the creature world, "Everything tempts," while from over here on our side, "even in the lightest things we waken counter-weight."

From this first leitmotif it would be only a step to the uncollected poems' total weave: rising and falling, remembering and forgetting, gazing and heartwork, consent and refusal, renunciation and intractability, shelter and exposure, departure and arrival, holding on and letting go—on and on, in seemingly endless refiguration. Perhaps it is unremarkable that the poems should possess so elaborate an inner architecture. After all, a single poet wrote them. But the meshwork feels more ardent than matter-of-fact. The sensation of a body of work is stronger than that of scattered moments of a life in crisis. And what this body of work gives us seems to come from a side of Rilke—one could even claim his strongest side—that is not otherwise apparent.

I have chosen to translate only a portion of the uncollected work. I have wanted to give a selection copious enough to convey a sense of the whole body of work—its scope, its variety, its temporal spread, especially its weave of motifs. But my primary goal has been to gather the *strongest* poems—at least those of the strongest that survive translation. Granted, this makes the selection partial in a double sense (Leishman's choice would have no doubt been different from mine). But I do feel that the poems selected here represent the uncollected work at its most formidable, and in its most ardent aspect. Such a gathering has seemed important, for reasons beyond adjusting our image of the later Rilke. Among the uncollected poems there seem to me at least a hundred that, if Rilke *had* published them together, would stand as one of the great volumes of poetry in twentieth-century literature.

I would like to express my debt to other translators of Rilke, especially J. B. Leishman, Rika Lesser, Michael Hamburger, Stephen Mitchell, Robert Bly, and Franz Wright. I would also like to thank Winifred Hamilton and Edward Hirsch for helping me with the introduction, and Cynthia MacDonald for lending moral support. Most of all, I would like to thank Michael Winkler for the many hours he spent talking with me about these poems, and for the many insights he shared with me.

UNCOLLECTED POEMS

Vergiß, vergiß und laß uns jetzt nur dies
erleben, wie die Sterne durch geklärten
Nachthimmel dringen; wie der Mond die Gärten
voll übersteigt. Wir fühlten längst schon, wies
spiegelnder wird im Dunkel; wie ein Schein
entsteht, ein weißer Schatten in dem Glanz
der Dunkelheit. Nun aber laß uns ganz
hinübertreten in die Welt hinein
die monden ist—

Forget, forget, and let us live now
only this, how the stars pierce through
cleared nocturnal sky; how the moon's whole disk
surmounts the gardens. We've sensed so long already
how the darkness breeds many mirrors: how a gleam
takes shape, a white shadow in the radiance
of night. But now let us cross over
and invest this world where
everything is lunar—

Paris, early summer 1909

Sag weißt du Liebesnächte? Treiben nicht
auf deinem Blut Kelchblätter weicher Worte?
Sind nicht an deinem lieben Leibe Orte,
die sich entsinnen wie ein Angesicht?

You don't know nights of love? Don't
petals of soft words float upon your blood?
Are there no places on your dear body
that keep remembering like eyes?

Paris, summer 1909

Scharfer Burgbruch, alter Unterkiefer
ausgehenkt aus dem Gebiß der Zeit
. . . .

Wann ist die Zeit, die diese Dinge mindert?
Ich wartete: doch nie zerbrach ein Stein.

Sharp castle-break, ancient underjaw
unhinged from the mouth of time
. . . .
When *is* the time through which these things erode?
I waited: but not one stone broke.

Les Baux, early October 1909

MONDNACHT

Weg in den Garten, tief wie ein langes Getränke,
leise im weichen Gezweig ein entgehender Schwung.
Oh und der Mond, der Mond, fast blühen die Bänke
von seiner zögernden Näherung.

Stille, wie drängt sie. Bist du jetzt oben erwacht?
Sternig und fühlend steht dir das Fenster entgegen.
Hände der Winde verlegen
an dein nahes Gesicht die entlegenste Nacht.

MOONLIT NIGHT

Path in the garden, deep as a long drink,
gently in soft branches gathering force and then gone.
Oh and the moon, the moon, the benches almost
blooming from its slow approach.

The silence, how it throngs. Are you awake up there?
Starry and full of feeling the window faces you.
Hands of the winds transpose to your near countenance
the remotest night.

Paris, beginning of July 1911

Schläfer, schwarz ist das Naß noch an meinen Füßen, ungenau.
Tau sagen sie. / Ach, daß ich Judith bin, herkomme von ihm, aus
dem Zelt aus dem Bett, austriefend sein Haupt, dreifach trunkenes
Blut. Weintrunken, trunken vom Räucherwerk, trunken von mir—
und jetzt nüchtern wie Tau. / Niedrig gehaltenes Haupt über dem
Morgengras; ich aber oben auf meinem Gang, ich Erhobene. / Plötz-
lich leeres Gehirn, abfließende Bilder ins Erdreich; mir aber quillend
ins Herz alle Breite der Nach-Tat. / Liebende, die ich bin. / Schrecken
trieben in mir alle Wonnen zusamm, an mir sind alle Stellen. / Herz,
mein berühmtes Herz, schlag an den Gegenwind:

wie ich geh, wie ich geh / und schneller die Stimme in mir, meine,
die rufen wird, Vogelruf, vor der Not-Stadt.

JUDITH'S RETURN

Sleepers, the damp on my feet is still black, indistinct. Dew they say. / Ah, that I am Judith, am coming from him, out of the tent out of the bed, out-trickling his head, three-times drunken blood. Wine-drunk, drunk with incense-work, drunk with me—and now sober as dew. / Low-held head over the morning grass; but I up above on my way, exalted. / Suddenly empty brain, draining-away images into the soil; but gushing into my heart all the breadth of the after-deed. / Woman in love that I am. / In me terrors have chased together all raptures, on me all places find their spot. / Heart, my renowned heart, beat on the countering wind:

how I stride, how I stride / and swifter the voice in me, mine that will call, birdcall, before the locked-in city of fear.

Paris, July 1911

[I]

Ich hielt mich überoffen, ich vergaß,
daß draußen nicht nur Dinge sind und voll
in sich gewohnte Tiere, deren Aug
aus ihres Lebens Rundung anders nicht
hinausreicht als ein eingerahmtes Bild;
daß ich in mich mit allem immerfort
Blicke hineinriß: Blicke, Meinung, Neugier.
    Wer weiß, es bilden Augen sich im Raum
und wohnen bei. Ach nur zu dir gestürzt,
ist mein Gesicht nicht ausgestellt, verwächst
in dich und setzt sich dunkel
unendlich fort in dein geschütztes Herz.

[II]

Wie man ein Tuch vor angehäuften Atem,
nein: wie man es an eine Wunde preßt,
aus der das Leben ganz, in einem Zug,
hinauswill, hielt ich dich an mich: ich sah,
du wurdest rot von mir. Wer spricht es aus,
was uns geschah? Wir holten jedes nach,
wozu die Zeit nie war. Ich reifte seltsam
in jedem Antrieb übersprungner Jugend,
und du, Geliebte, hattest irgendeine
wildeste Kindheit über meinem Herzen.

[III]

Entsinnen ist da nicht genug, es muß
von jenen Augenblicken pures Dasein
auf meinem Grunde sein, ein Niederschlag
der unermeßlich überfüllten Lösung.

TO LOU ANDREAS-SALOMÉ

I

I held myself too open, I forgot
that outside not just things exist and animals
fully at ease in themselves, whose eyes
reach from their lives' roundedness no differently
than portraits do from frames; forgot that I
with all I did incessantly crammed
looks into myself: looks, opinion, curiosity.
  Who knows: perhaps eyes form in space
and look on everywhere. Ah, only plunged toward you
does my face cease being on display, grows
into you and twines on darkly,
endlessly, into your sheltered heart.

II

As one puts a handkerchief before pent-in breath—
no: as one presses it against a wound
out of which the whole of life, in a single gush,
wants to stream, I held you to me: I saw
you turn red from me. How could anyone express
what took place between us? We made up for everything
there was never time for. I matured strangely
in every impulse of unperformed youth,
and you, love, somehow had
wildest childhood over my heart.

III

Memory won't suffice here: from those moments
there must be layers of pure existence
on my being's floor, a precipitate
from that immensely overfilled solution.

Denn ich *gedenke* nicht, das, was ich *bin*
rührt mich um deinetwillen. Ich erfinde
dich nicht an traurig ausgekühlten Stellen,
von wo du wegkamst; selbst, daß du nicht da bist,
ist warm von dir und wirklicher und mehr
als ein Entbehren. Sehnsucht geht zu oft
ins Ungenaue. Warum soll ich mich
auswerfen, während mir vielleicht dein Einfluß
leicht ist, wie Mondschein einem Platz am Fenster.

For I don't *think back*; all that I *am*
stirs me because of you. I don't invent you
at sadly cooled-off places from which
you've gone away; even your not being there
is warm with you and more real and more
than a privation. Longing leads out too often
into vagueness. Why should I cast myself,
when, for all I know, your influence falls on me,
gently, like moonlight on a window seat.

Duino, late autumn 1911

Perlen entrollen. Weh, riß eine der Schnüre?
Aber was hülf es, reih ich sie wieder: du fehlst mir,
starke Schließe, die sie verhielte, Geliebte.

War es nicht Zeit? Wie der Vormorgen den Aufgang,
wart ich dich an, blaß von geleisteter Nacht;
wie ein volles Theater, bild ich ein großes Gesicht,
daß deines hohen mittleren Auftritts
nichts mir entginge. O wie ein Golf hofft ins Offne
und vom gestreckten Leuchtturm
scheinende Räume wirft; wie ein Flußbett der Wüste,
daß es vom reinen Gebirg bestürze, noch himmlisch, der Regen,—
wie der Gefangne, aufrecht, die Antwort des einen
Sternes ersehnt, herein in sein schuldloses Fenster;
wie einer die warmen
Krücken sich wegreißt, daß man sie hin an den Altar
hänge, und daliegt und ohne Wunder nicht aufkann:
siehe, so wälz ich, wenn du nicht kommst, mich zu Ende.

Dich nur begehr ich. Muß nicht die Spalte im Pflaster,
wenn sie, armsälig, Grasdrang verspürt: muß sie den ganzen
Frühling nicht wollen? Siehe, den Frühling der Erde.
Braucht nicht der Mond, damit sich sein Abbild im Dorfteich
fände, des fremden Gestirns große Erscheinung? Wie kann
das Geringste geschehn, wenn nicht die Fülle der Zukunft,
alle vollzählige Zeit, sich uns entgegenbewegt?

Bist du nicht endlich in ihr, Unsägliche? Noch eine Weile,
und ich besteh dich nicht mehr. Ich altere oder dahin
bin ich von Kindern verdrängt . . .

Pearls roll away. Ah, one of the strings broke?
But what help would it be to rethread them: I lack you,
strong clasp, to hold them in place, beloved.

Was it not time? The way first morning waits for sunrise
I wait for you, pale with accomplished night;
like a packed theater, I coalesce into one great face
so that nothing of your high central entrance
will escape me. O as a gulf hopes into the Open
and out of the upstretched lighthouse
casts shining spaces; as a riverbed in the desert
craves from the pure mountains that rush, still heavenly, of rain,—
as the prisoner, standing, longs for the answer
of the one star to come in through his innocent window;
as a man rips the warm
crutches away so they can be hung on the altar,
and lies there and without a miracle will never rise:
so I shall writhe my way, unless you come, toward some end.

I crave only you. Must not the crack in the pavement,
when, in its wretchedness, it feels grass-surge: must it not
will the entire spring? Look, the *terrestrial* spring.
Does not the moon require the strange star's great shining
in order to find itself mirrored in the village pond?
How can the least thing happen, if the future's fullness,
all of time's great sum, does not move toward us?

Are you not finally in it, Unsayable? A while longer
and I shall cease to be up to you. I grow old, or else children
crowd me aside . . .

Begun Venice, early July 1912; completed in Spain, end of 1912

Ach, da wir Hülfe von Menschen erharrten: stiegen
Engel lautlos mit einem Schritte hinüber
über das liegende Herz

Ah, as we prayed for human help: angels soundlessly,
with single strides, climbed over
our prostrate hearts

Venice, July 11, 1912

O die Kurven meiner Sehnsucht durch das Weltall,
und auf jedem Streifen: meines Wesens
hingeschleudert. Manches nicht vor tausend
Jahren auf der wehn Ellipse seines
Schwunges wiederkommend und vorüber.
Eilend durch die einst gewesne Zukunft,
sich erkennend in den Jahreszeiten
oder luftig, als genauer Einfluß
beinah sternisch in den überwachen
Apparaten eine Weile bebend

O the curves of my longing through the cosmos,
and on all the streaks: my being's
flung-outness. Many an aspect returning
only after a thousand years on the sad ellipsis
of its momentum and passing on.
Hastening through the once-existent future,
knowing itself in the year's seasons
or airily, as an exact influence
almost starlike in the overwakeful
apparatus for a short time trembling

Venice, mid-July 1912

Komm wann du sollst. Dies alles wird durch mich
hindurchgegangen sein zu deinem Atem.
Ich habs, um deinetwillen, namenlos
lang angesehen mit dem Blick der Armut
und so geliebt als tränkst du es schon ein.

Und doch: bedenk ichs, daß ich dieses, mich,
Gestirne, Blumen und den schönen Wurf
der Vögel aus nachwinkendem Gesträuch,
der Wolken Hochmut und was nachts der Wind
mir antun konnte, mich aus einem Wesen
hinüberwandelnd in ein nächstes,—daß
ich eines nach dem andern, denn ich bins,
bin was der Tränke Rauschen mir im Ohr
zurückließ, bin der Wohlgeschmack, den einst
die schöne Frucht an meinen Lippen ausgab,—
daß ich dies alles, wenn du einmal da bist,
bis rückwärts zu des Kindes niederm Anblick
in Blumenkelche, da die Wiesen hochstehn,
ja bis zu einem Lächeln meiner Mutter
das ich vielleicht, gedrängt von deinem Dasein,
annehme wie Entwendetes—, daß ich
dann unerschöpflich Tag und Nacht soviel
entbehrend angeeignete Natur
hingeben sollte—, wissend nicht, ob das
was in dir aufglüht Meines ist: vielleicht
wirst du nur schöner, ganz aus eigner Schönheit
vom Überfluß der Ruh in deinen Gliedern,
vom Süßesten in deinem Blut, was weiß ich,
weil du dich selbst in deiner Hand erkennst,
weil dir das Haar an deinen Schultern schmeichelt,
weil irgendetwas in der dunkeln Luft
sich dir verständigt, weil du mich vergißt,
weil du nicht hinhörst, weil du eine Frau bist:

Come when you should. All this will have been
passing through me for you to breathe.
I have gazed at it for so long, for your sake,
namelessly, with the gaze of poverty,
and have loved it, as if already you drank it in.

And yet: when I recall that all this—
myself, stars, flowers, and the sharp flight
of a bird out of gesturing brushwood,
the clouds' haughtiness and what the wind
could do to me at night, whisking me
out of one being into a next,—that all this,
in endless succession (for I *am* all this,
am what the potion's roar left behind
in my ear, am that exquisite taste which once
a ripe fruit expended on my lips),—
that all this, when once you're really here,
all, even back to the boy's low gaze
into the chalices of high-grown flower fields,
even back to one of my mother's smiles
which I perhaps, thronged with your being,
shall think of as something stolen—, that all this
I then shall have to inexhaustibly outgive,
night and day, so much unsparingly
assimilated nature—, never knowing if what
begins to glow in you is mine: perhaps
you'll grow more beautiful entirely from your own beauty,
from the profusion of restedness in your limbs,
from what is sweetest in your blood,—for all I know,
because there is awareness even in your hand,
because your hair flatters your shoulders,
because something in the dark breeze
is one with you, because you forget me totally,
because you don't strain to hear, because you are a woman:

wenn ichs bedenke, wie ich Zärtlichkeit
getaucht ins Blut, ins nie von mir erschreckte
lautlose Herzblut so geliebter Dinge

when I recall how I've dipped tenderness
into blood, into that never startled
soundless heartblood of things so loved

Toledo, November 1912

Ich Wissender: oh der ich eingeweiht
in alles Handeln bin und mich nicht rühre,
fortwährend tritt der Held aus meiner Türe
hinausentschlossen, wie mit mir entzweit.

I, knower: possessing the secrets
of all action and not stirring,
while the hero strides out of my door
outward-resolved, as if breaking off with me.

Ronda, beginning of January 1913

Die Mandelbäume in Blüte: alles, was wir hier leisten können, ist, sich ohne Rest erkennen in der irdischen Erscheinung.

Unendlich staun ich euch an, ihr Seligen, euer Benehmen,
wie ihr die schwindliche Zier traget in ewigem Sinn.
Ach wers verstünde zu blühn: dem wär das Herz über alle
schwachen Gefahren hinaus und in der großen getrost.

The almond trees in bloom: the most we can achieve here is to know
ourselves unreservedly in our earthly appearance.

Always I marvel at you, you blessed ones,—at your demeanor,
the way you bear transient jewels with eternal ease.
Ah, if *we* knew how to blossom: our hearts would be out beyond
all lesser dangers, safe in the single great one.

Ronda, December 1912–January 1913

[I]

Aus dieser Wolke, siehe: die den Stern
so wild verdeckt, der eben war—(und mir),
aus diesem Bergland drüben, das jetzt Nacht,
Nachtwinde hat für eine Zeit—(und mir),
aus diesem Fluß im Talgrund, der den Schein
zerrissner Himmels-Lichtung fängt—(und mir);
aus mir und alledem ein einzig Ding
zu machen, Herr: aus mir und dem Gefühl,
mit dem die Herde, eingekehrt im Pferch,
das große dunkle Nichtmehrsein der Welt
ausatmend hinnimmt—, mir und jedem Licht
im Finstersein der vielen Häuser, Herr:
ein Ding zu machen; aus den Fremden, denn
nicht Einen kenn ich, Herr, und mir und mir
ein Ding zu machen; aus den Schlafenden,
den fremden alten Männern im Hospiz,
die wichtig in den Betten husten, aus
schlaftrunknen Kindern an so fremder Brust,
aus vielen Ungenaun und immer mir,
aus nichts als mir und dem, was ich nicht kenn,
das Ding zu machen, Herr Herr Herr, das Ding,
das welthaft-irdisch wie ein Meteor
in seiner Schwere nur die Summe Flugs
zusammennimmt: nichts wiegend als die Ankunft.

[II]

Warum muß einer gehn und fremde Dinge
so auf sich nehmen, wie vielleicht der Träger
den fremdlings mehr und mehr gefüllten Marktkorb
von Stand zu Stand hebt und beladen nachgeht
und kann nicht sagen: Herr, wozu das Gastmahl?

30

THE SPANISH TRILOGY

I

From this cloud—look: that so wildly covers
the star that just shone there—(and from me),
from these mountains across the way, which hold
night, nightwinds, for a while—(and from me),
from this stream on the valley's floor, which catches
the gleam of torn sky-clearings—(and from me);
from me and from all of this to make
a single thing, Lord: from me and those deep soughs
with which the herd, put up in the fold,
waits out the great dark cessation
of the world—, from me and from every candle
in the dimness of the many houses, Lord:
to make one thing; from the strangers, for I
don't know anyone, Lord, and from me and from me
to make *one* thing; from those sleeping,
the strange old men in the hospice
who cough out importantly in their beds,
from sleepdrunk children on so strange a breast,
from many vaguenesses and always from me,
from me alone and all I don't know,
to make the thing, Lord Lord Lord, the thing
that, cosmic-terrestrial, like a meteor
collects in its gravity only the sum of flight:
weighing nothing finally but arrival.

II

Why must a man go about and take unknown things
so much upon himself—as perhaps some porter
hefts from stall to stall the market basket
that keeps filling up, while he, weighed down, follows
and can never ask: Master, why this feast?

Warum muß einer dastehn wie ein Hirt,
so ausgesetzt dem Übermaß von Einfluß,
beteiligt so an diesem Raum voll Vorgang,
daß er gelehnt an einen Baum der Landschaft
sein Schicksal hätte, ohne mehr zu handeln.
Und hat doch nicht im viel zu großen Blick
die stille Milderung der Herde. Hat
nichts als Welt, hat Welt in jedem Aufschaun,
in jeder Neigung Welt. Ihm dringt, was andern
gerne gehört, unwirtlich wie Musik
und blind ins Blut und wandelt sich vorüber.

Da steht er nächtens auf und hat den Ruf
des Vogels draußen schon in seinem Dasein
und fühlt sich kühn, weil er die ganzen Sterne
in sein Gesicht nimmt, schwer—, o nicht wie einer,
der der Geliebten diese Nacht bereitet
und sie verwöhnt mit den gefühlten Himmeln.

[III]

Daß mir doch, wenn ich wieder der Städte Gedräng
und verwickelten Lärmknäul und die
Wirrsal des Fahrzeugs um mich habe, einzeln,
daß mir doch über das dichte Getrieb
Himmel erinnerte und der erdige Bergrand,
den von drüben heimwärts die Herde betrat.
Steinig sei mir zu Mut
und das Tagwerk des Hirten scheine mir möglich,
wie er einhergeht und bräunt und mit messendem Steinwurf
seine Herde besäumt, wo sie sich ausfranst.
Langsamen Schrittes, nicht leicht, nachdenklichen Körpers,
aber im Stehn ist er herrlich. Noch immer dürfte ein Gott
heimlich in diese Gestalt und würde nicht minder.

Why must a man stand here like a shepherd,
so exposed to the excess of influence,
involved so in this space full of happening
that merely leaning against a tree in the landscape
he would have his fate, nothing more to do.
And yet lacks in his far too open gaze
the quiet solace of the herd. Has
only world, world in each glance upward,
world each time his eyes bend down. What gladly
settles into others shoots through his blood like music—
blindly, inhospitably, changing and passing on.

At night then he gets up and has the call
of a bird outside already within him
and feels bold, since he takes all the stars
into his face, gravely—, O not like one
who shapes this night for his beloved
so he can pamper her with heartfilled skies.

III

But may I, when again I have the city's crush
and tangled noise-skein and furor
of its traffic wrapped around me, alone,
may I above that thick confusion
recall sky and the gentle mountain rim
on which the far-off plodding herd curved homeward.
May my spirit be like rock
and the shepherd's life seem conceivable—
the way he drifts and darkens and with measuring stonethrow
mends his flock, wherever it frays.
His steps slow, not light, his body pensive,
but in his standing-there, majestic. Even now a god might
slip into this form and not be lessened.

Abwechselnd weilt er und zieht, wie selber der Tag,
und Schatten der Wolken
durchgehn ihn, als dächte der Raum
langsam Gedanken für ihn.

Sei er wer immer für euch. Wie das wehende Nachtlicht
in den Mantel der Lampe stell ich mich innen in ihn.
Ein Schein wird ruhig. Der Tod
fände sich reiner zurecht.

Alternately he moves and lingers, like the day itself,
and the shadows of the clouds
pass through him, as though space were slowly
thinking thoughts for him.

Make of him whom you will. Like a wind-whipped nightflame
into the lamp's mantle I place myself inside him.
A flare grows steady. Might Death
less darkly find its way.

Ronda, early January 1913

Also, das tat not für den und den,
weil sie Zeichen brauchten, welche schrieen.
Doch er träumte, Marthen und Marieen
müßte es genügen, einzusehn,
daß er *könne*. Aber keiner glaubte,
alle sprachen: Herr, was kommst du *nun?*
Und da ging er hin, das Unerlaubte
an der ruhigen Natur zu tun.
Zürnender. Die Augen fast geschlossen,
fragte er sie nach dem Grab. Er litt.
Ihnen schien es, seine Tränen flossen,
und sie drängten voller Neugier mit.
Noch im Gehen wars ihm ungeheuer,
ein entsetzlich spielender Versuch,
aber plötzlich brach ein hohes Feuer
in ihm aus, ein solcher Widerspruch
gegen alle ihre Unterschiede,
ihr Gestorben-, ihr Lebendigsein,
daß er Feindschaft war in jedem Gliede,
als er heiser angab: Hebt den Stein!
Eine Stimme rief, daß er schon stinke,
(denn er lag den vierten Tag)—doch Er
stand gestrafft, ganz voll von jenem Winke,
welcher stieg in ihm und schwer, sehr schwer
ihm die Hand hob—(niemals hob sich eine
langsamer als diese Hand und mehr)
bis sie dastand, scheinend in der Luft;
und dort oben zog sie sich zur Kralle:
denn ihn graute jetzt, es möchten alle
Toten durch die angesaugte Gruft
wiederkommen, wo es sich herauf
raffte, larvig, aus der graden Lage—
doch dann stand nur Eines schief im Tage,

THE RAISING OF LAZARUS

Yes, it was necessary for this common sort,
since they required signs, signs that screamed.
Yet he dreamt how for Martha and Mary
it would be enough simply to see
that he *could*. But none of them believed,
they all said to him: Lord, why come *now*?
And so he went, to do the unallowed
to peaceful Nature.
In anger. His eyes almost shut,
he asked where the grave was. Tormentedly.
It seemed to them that his tears streamed,
and they thronged behind him, full of curiosity.
Even on the way he thought it monstrous,
an appalling, frivolous experiment,
but suddenly a great fire broke out in him,
such an argument
against their prized distinctions,
their death and life, their here and there,
that he was enmity in every limb
when he instructed hoarsely: Lift the stone!
A voice shouted that he must stink by now
(for he'd lain there four days)—but He
stood tensed, entirely filled with that gesture
which rose in him and heavily, so heavily
lifted his hand—(no hand ever raised itself
this slowly, with this much weight)
until it stood there, shining in the air;
and then it clenched almost clawlike:
for now he dreaded that all the dead might
come rushing back through the suction
of that tomb, where the thing had started
to writhe up, larva-like, from its stiff reclining—
but then just a single shape stood there,

und man sah: das ungenaue vage
Leben nahm es wieder mit in Kauf.

crooked in the daylight, and one witnessed:
the inexact vague Life again accept it.

Ronda, January 1913

DER GEIST ARIEL

(Nach der Lesung von Shakespeares Sturm)

Man hat ihn einmal irgendwo befreit
mit jenem Ruck, mit dem man sich als Jüngling
ans Große hinriß, weg von jeder Rücksicht.
Da ward er willens, sieh: und seither dient er,
nach jeder Tat gefaßt auf seine Freiheit.
Und halb sehr herrisch, halb beinah verschämt,
bringt mans ihm vor, daß man für dies und dies
ihn weiter brauche, ach, und muß es sagen,
was man ihm half. Und dennoch fühlt man selbst,
wie alles das, was man mit ihm zurückhält,
fehlt in der Luft. Verführend fast und süß:
ihn hinzulassen—, um dann, nicht mehr zaubernd,
ins Schicksal eingelassen wie die andern,
zu wissen, daß sich seine leichte Freundschaft,
jetzt ohne Spannung, nirgends mehr verpflichtet,
ein Überschuß zu dieses Atmens Raum,
gedankenlos im Element beschäftigt.
Abhängig fürder, länger nicht begabt,
den dumpfen Mund zu jenem Ruf zu formen,
auf den er stürzte. Machtlos, alternd, arm
und doch *ihn* atmend wie unfaßlich weit
verteilten Duft, der erst das Unsichtbare
vollzählig macht. Auflächelnd, daß man dem
so winken durfte, in so großen Umgang
so leicht gewöhnt. Aufweinend vielleicht auch,
wenn man bedenkt, wie's einen liebte und
fortwollte, beides, immer ganz in Einem.

(Ließ ich es schon? Nun schreckt mich dieser Mann,
der wieder Herzog wird. Wie er sich sanft
den Draht ins Haupt zieht und sich zu den andern
Figuren hängt und künftighin das Spiel
um Milde bittet. . . . Welcher Epilog

THE SPIRIT ARIEL
(After reading Shakespeare's Tempest*)*

Once long ago somewhere you freed him
with that same jolt with which as a young man
you tore yourself toward greatness, away from all regard.
Then he grew willing, and ever since he serves,
after each deed poised for freedom.
And half imperiously, half almost ashamed,
you inform him that for this and that
you still require him, and, ah, must tell again
that story of how you helped him. And yet you feel, yourself,
how everything that you keep back through him
is missing from the air. How sweet and almost tempting:
to let him go—, and then, no longer conjuring,
enrolled in fate like all the others,
to know that his light friendship,
without strain now, nowhere any obligation,
a surplus to this breathing's space,
is at work in the element, thoughtlessly.
Henceforth dependent, no longer with that gift
to shape the dull mouth into that call
at which he came. Powerless, aging, poor
and yet breathing *him* like incomprehensibly far-flung
allotted fragrance by which alone the invisible
is made complete. Smiling, that you could
summon him so, in such great dealings
so easily at home. Perhaps weeping too,
when you remember how it loved you and
longed to leave, both, always the same urge.

(Have I let it go? Now this man frightens me,
who is becoming Duke again. How gently
he draws the wire through his own head and hangs
himself up with the other figures and begs
henceforth the play's indulgence . . . What an epilogue

vollbrachter Herrschaft. Abtun, bloßes Dastehn
mit nichts als eigner Kraft: »und das ist wenig.«)

to lordship consummated. Mere naked standing-there
with nothing but his own strength: "which is most faint.")

Ronda, January–February 1913

So angestrengt wider die starke Nacht
werfen sie ihre Stimmen ins Gelächter,
das schlecht verbrennt. O aufgelehnte Welt
voll Weigerung. Und atmet doch den Raum,
in dem die Sterne gehen. Siehe, dies
bedürfte nicht und könnte, der Entfernung
fremd hingegeben, in dem Übermaß
von Fernen sich ergehen, fort von uns.
Und nun geruhts und reicht uns ans Gesicht
wie der Geliebten Aufblick; schlägt sich auf
uns gegenüber und zerstreut vielleicht
an uns sein Dasein. Und wir sinds nicht wert.
Vielleicht entziehts den Engeln etwas Kraft,
daß nach uns her der Sternenhimmel nachgiebt
und uns hereinhängt ins getrübte Schicksal.
Umsonst. Denn wer gewahrts? Und wo es einer
gewärtig wird: wer darf noch an den Nacht-Raum
die Stirne lehnen wie ans eigne Fenster?
Wer hat dies nicht verleugnet? Wer hat nicht
in dieses eingeborne Element
gefälschte, schlechte, nachgemachte Nächte
hereingeschleppt und sich daran begnügt?
Wir lassen Götter stehn um gohren Abfall,
denn Götter locken nicht. Sie haben Dasein
und nichts als Dasein, Überfluß von Dasein,
doch nicht Geruch, nicht Wink. Nichts ist so stumm
wie eines Gottes Mund. Schön wie ein Schwan
auf seiner Ewigkeit grundlosen Fläche:
so zieht der Gott und taucht und schont sein Weiß.

Alles verführt. Der kleine Vogel selbst
tut Zwang an uns aus seinem reinen Laubwerk,
die Blume hat nicht Raum und drängt herüber;
was will der Wind nicht alles? Nur der Gott,

Straining so hard against the strength of night
they cast their voices into that laughter
that will not flame. O obstinate world
full of refusal. And yet breathing the space
in which the stars move. Look, all this
needs nothing and could, having pledged itself
to distance, roam through the deepest
regions of remoteness, far from us.
And deigns now to touch our faces
as does the loved one's sudden glance; opens
before us and perhaps lavishes
its being on us. And we aren't worth it.
Perhaps it extracts power from the angels,
so that the starry sky will bend toward us
and suspend itself inside our murky fate.
In vain. For who takes note? And even where
someone does: who dares to lean his brow
against nightspace as against his own window?
Who hasn't disavowed all this? Who hasn't
hauled counterfeited, third-rate, mimic nights
into this inborn element of ours
and been content with that?
We're drawn away from gods toward rotting refuse,
for gods do not entice. They possess being
and only being, great stores of being,
but not scent, not gesture. Nothing is so silent
as a god's mouth. Serenely, like a swan
on its eternity of unplumbed surface:
the god glides and dives and saves his whiteness.

Everything tempts. Even the small bird,
from its pure leafwork, exerts force on us;
the flower has no space and presses over;
what would the wind *not* have? Only the god,

wie eine Säule, läßt vorbei, verteilend
hoch oben, wo er trägt, nach beiden Seiten
die leichte Wölbung seines Gleichmuts.

like a column, lets pass, distributing
high up, where he supports, toward either side
the light arch of his equanimity.

Paris, end of February 1913

Wir wissen nicht, was wir verbringen: siehe,
Benanntes ist vorbei und jedes Sein
erfindet sich im letzten Augenblick
und will nichts hören / Wink von Zeichen, kaum
ein Blatt verkehrts: wir aber sind schon anders,
verleugnen, lächeln, kennen schon nicht mehr,
was gestern Glück war. Und die Göttin selbst
schwankt über uns.

We don't know what we spend:
all that's named is past and each being
invents itself at the last second
and will hear nothing / Hint of signals,
one leaf barely turned; but by now we've changed,
we disavow, smile, already lack all sense
of yesterday's good fortune. And the goddess herself
sways over us.

Paris, beginning of March 1913

Lange mußt du leiden, kennend nicht was,
bis plötzlich aus gehässig erbissener Frucht
deines Leidens Geschmack eintritt in dir.
Und da liebst du schon fast das Gekostete. Keiner
redet dirs wieder aus

Long you must suffer, knowing not what,
until suddenly out of spitefully chewed fruit
your suffering's taste comes forth in you.
Then you will love almost instantly what's tasted. No one
will ever talk you out of it

Paris, March 1913

Weißt du nicht, wird der Rotdorn bald
unser Gefühl bemühn?
Leise steigt das Grün.
Plötzlich hebt sich die Blühgestalt.
Ach, da klagen in dir
die du immer ins Zimmer gestellt
viele Blumen.

The hawthorn there: who would guess
that it will soon be clamoring at our feelings.
The green climbs softly.
Suddenly the red flowershape lifts up.
Ah, there lament in you—
you who had to have them in your room—
so many flowers.

Paris, March 1913

Unwissend vor dem Himmel meines Lebens,
anstaunend steh ich. O die großen Sterne.
Aufgehendes und Niederstieg. Wie still.
Als wär ich nicht. Nehm ich denn Teil? Entriet ich
dem reinen Einfluß? Wechselt Flut und Ebbe
in meinem Blut nach dieser Ordnung? Abtun
will ich die Wünsche, jeden andern Anschluß,
mein Herz gewöhnen an sein Fernstes. Besser
es lebt im Schrecken seiner Sterne, als
zum Schein beschützt, von einer Näh beschwichtigt.

Unknowing before the heavens of my life
I stand in wonder. O the great stars.
The rising and the going down. How quiet.
As if I didn't exist. *Am* I part? Have I dismissed
the pure influence? Do high and low tide
alternate in my blood according to this order?
I will cast off all wishes, all other links,
accustom my heart to its remotest space. Better
it live in the terror of its stars than
seemingly protected, soothed by something near.

Paris, early 1913

Überfließende Himmel verschwendeter Sterne
prachten über der Kümmernis. Statt in die Kissen,
weine hinauf. Hier, an dem weinenden schon,
an dem endenden Antlitz,
um sich greifend, beginnt der hin-
reißende Weltraum. Wer unterbricht,
wenn du dort hin drängst,
die Strömung? Keiner. Es sei denn,
daß du plötzlich ringst mit der gewaltigen Richtung
jener Gestirne nach dir. Atme.
Atme das Dunkel der Erde und wieder
aufschau! Wieder. Leicht und gesichtlos
lehnt sich von oben Tiefe dir an. Das gelöste
nachtenthaltne Gesicht giebt dem deinigen Raum.

Overflowing heavens of squandered stars
flame brilliantly above your troubles. Instead
of into your pillows, weep up toward them.
There, at the already weeping, at the ending visage,
slowly thinning out, ravishing
worldspace begins. Who will interrupt,
once you force your way there,
the current? No one. You may panic,
and fight that overwhelming course of stars
that streams toward you. Breathe.
Breathe the darkness of the earth and again
look up! Again. Lightly and facelessly
depths lean toward you from above. The serene
countenance dissolved in night makes room for yours.

Paris, April 1913

Narziss verging. Von seiner Schönheit hob
sich unaufhörlich seines Wesens Nähe,
verdichtet wie der Duft vom Heliotrop.
Ihm aber war gesetzt, daß er sich sähe.

Er liebte, was ihm ausging, wieder ein
und war nicht mehr im offnen Wind enthalten
und schloß entzückt den Umkreis der Gestalten
und hob sich auf und konnte nicht mehr sein.

NARCISSUS [1]

Narcissus vanished. His beauty gave off
incessantly the fragrance of his being,
heightened like the scent from heliotrope.
But for him self-seeing was the task.

Whatever escaped him he loved back in,
and was borne no longer in the open breeze
and closed raptly the radius of forms
and eclipsed himself and could exist no more.

Paris, April 1913

Dies also: dies geht von mir aus und löst
sich in der Luft und im Gefühl der Haine,
entweicht mir leicht und wird nicht mehr das Meine
und glänzt, weil es auf keine Feindschaft stößt.

Dies hebt sich unaufhörlich von mir fort,
ich will nicht weg, ich warte, ich verweile;
doch alle meine Grenzen haben Eile,
stürzen hinaus und sind schon dort.

Und selbst im Schlaf. Nichts bindet uns genug.
Nachgiebige Mitte in mir, Kern voll Schwäche,
der nicht sein Fruchtfleisch anhält. Flucht, o Flug
von allen Stellen meiner Oberfläche.

Was sich dort bildet und mir sicher gleicht
und aufwärts zittert in verweinten Zeichen,
das mochte so in einer Frau vielleicht
innen entstehn; es war nicht zu erreichen,

wie ich danach auch drängend in sie rang.
Jetzt liegt es offen in dem teilnahmslosen
zerstreuten Wasser, und ich darf es lang
anstaunen unter meinem Kranz von Rosen.

Dort ist es nicht geliebt. Dort unten drin
ist nichts, als Gleichmut überstürzter Steine,
und ich kann sehen, wie ich traurig bin.
War dies mein Bild in ihrem Augenscheine?

Hob es sich so in ihrem Traum herbei
zu süßer Furcht? Fast fühl ich schon die ihre.

NARCISSUS [II]

And this: this escapes from me and dissolves
in the air and in the aura of the grove,
leaves me softly and becomes mine no longer
and gleams, because it meets no enmity.

This rises incessantly away from me,
I try to stay, I wait, I linger;
but all my borders hasten elsewhere,
rush out and even now are *there*.

In sleep also. Nothing binds us in.
Pliant core in me, kernel full of weakness
that can't control its fruitflesh.
Fleeing, O flight from all places on my surface.

What forms down there and must resemble me
and quivers up in bleary outlines,—
it might have taken shape that way inside
a woman; but I could not attain it

as I struggled toward it pressing into her.
Now it lies open in the apathetic
scattered water, and I can gaze at it
for ages under my wreath of roses.

It is not loved there. Down there is nothing
but the equanimity of tumbled stones,
and I can see my sadness.
Was this my image in her eyes' flashing?

Did it surge into her dream like this
as some sweet fear? I can almost feel her fright.

Denn, wie ich mich in meinem Blick verliere:
ich könnte denken, daß ich tödlich sei.

For as I lose myself inside my gaze:
I could think that I am deadly.

Paris, April 1913

CHRISTI HÖLLENFAHRT

Endlich verlitten, entging sein Wesen dem schrecklichen
Leibe der Leiden. Oben. Ließ ihn.
Und die Finsternis fürchtete sich allein
und warf an das Bleiche
Fledermäuse heran,—immer noch schwankt abends
in ihrem Flattern die Angst vor dem Anprall
an die erkaltete Qual. Dunkle ruhlose Luft
entmutigte sich an dem Leichnam; und in den starken
wachsamen Tieren der Nacht war Dumpfheit und Unlust.
Sein entlassener Geist gedachte vielleicht in der Landschaft
anzustehen, unhandelnd. Denn seiner Leidung Ereignis
war noch genug. Maßvoll
schien ihm der Dinge nächtliches Dastehn,
und wie ein trauriger Raum griff er darüber um sich.
Aber die Erde, vertrocknet im Durst seiner Wunden,
aber die Erde riß auf, und es rufte im Abgrund.
Er, Kenner der Martern, hörte die Hölle
herheulend, begehrend Bewußtsein
seiner vollendeten Not: daß über dem Ende der seinen
(unendlichen) ihre, während Pein erschrecke, ahne.
Und er stürzte, der Geist, mit der völligen Schwere
seiner Erschöpfung herein: schritt als ein Eilender
durch das befremdete Nachschaun weidender Schatten,
hob zu Adam den Aufblick, eilig,
eilte hinab, schwand, schien und verging in dem Stürzen
wilderer Tiefen. Plötzlich (höher höher) über der Mitte
aufschäumender Schreie, auf dem langen
Turm seines Duldens trat er hervor: ohne Atem,
stand, ohne Geländer, Eigentümer der Schmerzen. Schwieg.

CHRIST'S DESCENT INTO HELL

Finally suffered-out, his being exited the terrible
body of pain. Up there. Left it.
And the darkness, abandoned, grew afraid,
and at the pallor
cast bats (even now in their nightfall swervings
one can see the fear of impact
with that chilled anguish). Dark restless air
grew disheartened near the corpse; and in the strong
watchful animals of the night there was dullness and torpor.
His released spirit thought perhaps to bide its time
in the landscape, inactive. For the extremes of his suffering
still throbbed in him. There was measure, he thought,
in the nocturnal standing-there of things,
and like a saddened space he began groping all around it.
But the earth, parched in the thirst of his wounds,
the earth ripped open, and there were calls in its chasm.
He, expert in agony, heard Hell howling toward him,
craving knowledge that his pain was finished:
envisioning—such horror!—beyond the end of his torment
(boundless), its own stretching on forever.
And he, the spirit now, plunged into it with the full weight
of his exhaustion: strode as one hastening
through the puzzled backward stare of pasturing shades,
raised his glance toward Adam, hastily,
hurried down, vanished, gleamed briefly, and dissolved in the
        plunging
of wilder depths. Suddenly (higher higher) over the center
of foaming screams, he stepped out onto the tall
tower of his endurance; without breathing,
stood, no handhold, possessor of pains. Was silent.

Paris, April 1913

Nun wachen wir mit den Erinnerungen
und halten das Gesicht an das, was war;
flüsternde Süße, die uns einst durchdrungen,
sitzt schweigend neben mit gelöstem Haar

Now we wake up with our memory
and fix our gazes on that which was;
whispering sweetness, which once coursed through us,
sits silently beside us with loosened hair

Paris, May 1913

Dich aufdenkend wird mein Wesen erglühter,
meine Adern röten die Nacht.
An meinem Herzen der gerüstete Hüter
klirrt vor Verdacht. Wacht
dein Gefühl durch die mündigen Sterne herüber?
Gehst du aus unaufhaltsamem Raum

Imagining you my being burns more brightly,
my veins turn the night red.
About my heart the armed guardian
rattles with suspicion. Has your feeling
caught sight of me down through the liberated stars?
Are you *coming* from unopposable space

Paris, May 1913

Bestürz mich, Musik, mit rhythmischem Zürnen!
Hoher Vorwurf, dicht vor dem Herzen erhoben,
das nicht so wogend empfand, das sich schonte. Mein Herz: *da:*
sieh deine Herrlichkeit. Hast du fast immer Genüge,
minder zu schwingen? Aber die Wölbungen warten,
die obersten, daß du sie füllst mit orgelndem Andrang.
Was ersehnst du der fremden Geliebten verhaltenes Antlitz?—
Hat deine Sehnsucht nicht Atem, aus der Posaune des Engels,
der das Weltgericht anbricht, tönende Stürme zu stoßen:
oh, so *ist* sie auch nicht, nirgends, wird nicht geboren,
die du verdorrend entbehrst . . .

Assault me, music, with rhythmic fury!
Lofty reproach, hurled up high before the heart
that didn't feel so surgingly, that spared itself. My heart: *there*:
behold your glory. Can you almost always make do
with lesser pulsings? —But the arches wait,
the uppermost, to be filled with thundering onrush.
Why do you long for the unknown loved one's withheld face?—
Has your craving not breath to blast echoing storms
from that angel's trumpet who announces the world's judgment:
then she too does not exist, *is* nowhere, will not be born,
she whose absence you parchingly endure . . .

Paris, May 1913

Hinter den schuld-losen Bäumen
langsam bildet die alte Verhängnis
ihr stummes Gesicht aus.
Falten ziehen dorthin . . .
Was ein Vogel hier aufkreischt,
springt dort als Weh-Zug
ab an dem harten Wahrsagermund.

O und die bald Liebenden
lächeln sich an, noch abschiedslos,
unter und auf über ihnen geht
sternbildhaft ihr Schicksal,
nächtig begeistert.
Noch zu erleben nicht reicht es sich ihnen,
noch wohnt es
schwebend im himmlischen Gang,
eine leichte Figur.

Behind the innocent trees
old Doom is slowly building up
her mute countenance.
Wrinkles make their way there . . .
What a bird shrieks here
leaps out there as a line of woe
on the hard soothsayer's lips.

O and the soon-to-be lovers
smile on each other, still farewell-less,
their destiny setting and rising
over them constellationlike,
happy in nightspace.
Yet to be lived it doesn't stretch toward them,
it still dwells
nestled in the celestial motion,
a ghostly outline.

Heiligendamm, August 1913

Wie junge Wiesen, blumig, einen Abhang
durch einen leichten Überzug von Wachstum
teilnehmend machen am Gefühl des Jahres,
windwissend, fühlend, milde, beinah glücklich
über des Bergs gefährlich-schräger Bildung:
so ruht Gesicht, hinblühend, mildvergänglich
auf dieses Schädels Vorderflächen, die,
absteigend, wie mit eines Weinbergs Neigung,
zum All sich halten, Strahlendem gegenüber.

Wie die Eichel in ihrem Becher, so ruhte diesem becherig fassenden
Haupte von oben die Krone ein: es war ein Teil von ihr, sie bildeten
zusammen ein einziges Stück Herrschaft, die Frucht König die der
Himmel zur Süße brachte. (Ein so leicht auf seinen Kern gelegtes
Gesicht, kaum mehr als die Einteilung des Gnomons auf schwerem
schrägem Stein. Gesicht, lautlos abfließend, oh Weinberg, von der
Schräge des Skeletts, breite ganz niedere Stirn, über deren ersten
Streifen schon die Krone Besitz ergreift; flügeliges Abstehen der
geistig-feinen Ohren. Der Bacchos eines inneren Weines. Gesicht,
dessen konstruktive Bedingungen mit seiner Verwendung überein-
stimmten, so daß sie aus sich selbst, ohne Zutat, zum reinsten Aus-
druck wurden. Ausdrücklichkeit des Mundes. Oberlippe über der
unteren, wie die Göttin, die den Himmel abhebt, von der Erde sich
wegbiegend. Aufruhen ihres reinen Schwunges auf der vorge-
schobenen Fülle der unteren Lippe. Leichtes Eingezeichnetsein der
oberen Züge, des flachen Auges, der groß tragenden Augenbogen,
gegen das Ausgeführtsein im Munde; die Nase giebt den Übergang
mit ihren rein sinnlich auseinander gestellten Flügeln.) (Vorläufig)

HEAD OF AMENOPHIS IV IN BERLIN

As young meadows, flowerfilled, through
a light blanket of new growth cause a slope
to take part in the feelings of the year,
windknowing, sentient, gentle, almost happy
over the mountain's slant-perilous form:
so this visage, bloomprofuse, gently transient,
rests on its skull's anteriors, which,
descending, as with a vineyard's contours,
jut out into the cosmos, all radiance everywhere.

As the acorn in its cup, so the crown nestled from above in the cuplike containing head: it was a part of it, they formed together a single piece of rulership, the king-fruit that Heaven brought to sweetness. (A face laid so lightly on its core, scarcely more than the distribution of the gnomon on heavy slanting stone. Face, soundlessly flowing away—oh vineyard—from the slope of the skeleton; broad, quite low forehead, over whose first stria the crown already takes possession; winglike protrusion of the finely intellectual ears. The Bacchus of an interior wine. Face, whose structural prerequisites coincided with the reason for its being, so that of themselves, without supplement, they grew to the purest expression. Expressiveness of the mouth. Upper lip above the lower like the goddess who lifts Heaven's rim, bending away from Earth. Onresting of its pure élan on the outthrust fullness of the lower lip. Light insketchedness of the upper features, of the shallow eyes, of the great supporting eyebrow-arches, in contrast to the outward elaboration in the mouth; the nose defines the transition point with the purely sensual separation of its nostrils.) (Provisional)

Late summer or autumn 1913

Wie das Gestirn, der Mond, erhaben, voll Anlaß,
plötzlich die Höhn übertritt, die entworfene Nacht
gelassen vollendend: siehe: so steigt mir
rein die Stimme hervor aus Gebirgen des Nichtmehr.
Und die Stellen, erstaunt, an denen du dawarst und fortkamst,
schmerzen klarer dir nach.

The way that bright planet, the moon, exalted, full of purpose,
all at once surmounts the peaks, filling in serenely
the outlined night: look: just so my voice
rises purely out of the mountains of nevermore.
And the places—awestruck—that you occupied and left
ache more clearly for you.

Autumn 1913

Tränen, Tränen, die aus mir brechen.
Mein Tod, Mohr, Träger
meines Herzens, halte mich schräger,
daß sie abfließen. Ich will sprechen.

Schwarzer, riesiger Herzhalter.
Wenn ich auch spräche,
glaubst du denn, daß das Schweigen bräche?

Wiege mich, Alter.

Tears, tears that break out of me.
My death, great Moor, bearer
of my heart, hold me at a slant
so they'll run off. I want to speak.

Black, gigantic heart-holder.
Even if I were to speak,
do you think the silence would break?

Cradle me, old man.

Paris, late autumn 1913

Einmal nahm ich zwischen meine Hände
dein Gesicht. Der Mond fiel darauf ein.
Unbegreiflichster der Gegenstände
unter überfließendem Gewein.

Wie ein williges, das still besteht,
beinah war es wie ein Ding zu halten.
Und doch war kein Wesen in der kalten
Nacht, das mir unendlicher entgeht.

O da strömen wir zu diesen Stellen,
drängen in die kleine Oberfläche
alle Wellen unsres Herzens,
Lust und Schwäche,
und wem halten wir sie schließlich hin?

Ach dem Fremden, der uns mißverstanden,
ach dem andern, den wir niemals fanden,
denen Knechten, die uns banden,
Frühlingswinden, die damit entschwanden,
und der Stille, der Verliererin.

Once I took your face into
my hands. Moonlight fell on it.
Most incomprehensible object
under overflowing tears.

Like something docile, that quietly endures,
it felt almost the way a thing feels.
And yet there was no being in that chill
night, which endlessly eludes me.

O these places toward which we surge,
pushing into the scant surfaces
all the waves of our heart,
our pleasures and our weaknesses,
and to whom do we finally hold them out?

To the stranger, who misunderstood us,
to the other, whom we never found,
to those slaves, who bound us,
to the spring winds, which promptly vanished,
and to silence, that spendthrift.

Paris, end of 1913

DIE GROSSE NACHT

Oft anstaunt ich dich, stand an gestern begonnenem Fenster,
stand und staunte dich an. Noch war mir die neue
Stadt wie verwehrt, und die unüberredete Landschaft
finsterte hin, als wäre ich nicht. Nicht gaben die nächsten
Dinge sich Müh, mir verständlich zu sein. An der Laterne
drängte die Gasse herauf: ich sah, daß sie fremd war.
Drüben—ein Zimmer, mitfühlbar, geklärt in der Lampe—,
schon nahm ich teil; sie empfandens, schlossen die Läden.
Stand. Und dann weinte ein Kind. Ich wußte die Mütter
rings in den Häusern, was sie vermögen—, und wußte
alles Weinens zugleich die untröstlichen Gründe.
Oder es sang eine Stimme und reichte ein Stück weit
aus der Erwartung heraus, oder es hustete unten
voller Vorwurf ein Alter, als ob sein Körper im Recht sei
wider die mildere Welt. Dann schlug eine Stunde—,
aber ich zählte zu spät, sie fiel mir vorüber.—
Wie ein Knabe, ein fremder, wenn man endlich ihn zuläßt,
doch den Ball nicht fängt und keines der Spiele
kann, die die andern so leicht an einander betreiben,
dasteht und wegschaut,—wohin—?: stand ich und plötzlich,
daß *du* umgehst mit mir, spielest, begriff ich, erwachsene
Nacht, und staunte dich an. Wo die Türme
zürnten, wo abgewendeten Schicksals
eine Stadt mich umstand und nicht zu erratende Berge
wider mich lagen, und im genäherten Umkreis
hungernde Fremdheit umzog das zufällige Flackern
meiner Gefühle—: da war es, du Hohe,
keine Schande für dich, daß du mich kanntest. Dein Atem
ging über mich. Dein auf weite Ernste verteiltes
Lächeln trat in mich ein.

THE GREAT NIGHT

Often I stared at you, stood at the window begun yesterday,
stood and stared at you in wonder. As yet the new
city was as if denied me, and the unpersuaded landscape
grew dark as if I didn't exist. The nearest things
took no care to make themselves known to me. The street
thrust up to the lamppost: I saw it was alien.
Across the way—a room, inviting, clear in the lamplight—,
already I was taking part; they sensed it, pulled the shutters closed.
I stood. And then a child cried. I felt the mothers
all around in the houses, the power they had,
and at the same time all crying's inconsolable ground.
Or a voice sang and reached a little beyond
expectation, or down below an old man coughed
full of reproach, as though his body were in the right
against the gentler world. Then an hour struck—,
but I counted too late, it tumbled past me.—
The way a boy, a new one, when at last he's chosen,
drops the first ball and gets lost in those games
the others pursue together with such ease
and stands there and gazes off,—to where—?: I stood
and suddenly felt *you* befriending me, *you* playing, grownup
night, and I stared at you in wonder. Where the towers
raged, where the lost fate of a city
stood around me and not-to-be-fathomed mountains
camped against me, and Strangeness, hungering,
circled in on the random flares
of my feeling—: it was then that you, in your greatness,
no trace of shame, acknowledged me. Your breath
passed over me. Your smile, spanning vast
solemnities, entered into me.

Paris, January 1914

Hebend die Blicke vom Buch, von den nahen zählbaren Zeilen,
in die vollendete Nacht hinaus:
O wie sich sternegemäß die gedrängten Gefühle verteilen,
so als bände man auf
einen Bauernstrauß:

Jugend der leichten und neigendes Schwanken der schweren
und der zärtlichen zögernder Bug—.
Überall Lust zu Bezug und nirgends Begehren;
Welt zu viel und Erde genug.

Looking up from my book, from the close countable lines,
into the finished-full night outside:
how in starry measure my packed feelings scatter,
as though a bouquet of wildflowers
were being untied:

youth of the light ones and bending sway of the heavy ones
and the tender ones' hesitant curve—.
Everywhere joy in relation and nowhere any craving;
world in excess and earth sufficient.

Paris, February 1914

Du im Voraus
verlorne Geliebte, Nimmergekommene,
nicht weiß ich, welche Töne dir lieb sind.
Nicht mehr versuch ich, dich, wenn das Kommende wogt,
zu erkennen. Alle die großen
Bilder in mir, im Fernen erfahrene Landschaft,
Städte und Türme und Brücken und un-
vermutete Wendung der Wege
und das Gewaltige jener von Göttern
einst durchwachsenen Länder:
steigt zur Bedeutung in mir
deiner, Entgehende, an.

Ach, die Gärten bist du,
ach, ich sah sie mit solcher
Hoffnung. Ein offenes Fenster
im Landhaus—, und du tratest beinahe
mir nachdenklich heran. Gassen fand ich,—
du warst sie gerade gegangen,
und die Spiegel manchmal der Läden der Händler
waren noch schwindlich von dir und gaben erschrocken
mein zu plötzliches Bild.—Wer weiß, ob derselbe
Vogel nicht hinklang durch uns
gestern, einzeln, im Abend?

You the beloved
lost in advance, you the never-arrived,
I don't know what songs you like most.
No longer, when the future crests toward the present,
do I try to discern you. All the great
images in me—the landscape experienced far off,
cities and towers and bridges and un-
suspected turns in the path
and the forcefulness of those lands
once intertwined with gods:
all mount up in me to signify
you, who forever eludes.

Ah, you are the gardens!
With such hope I
watched them! An open window
in the country house—, and you almost
stepped out pensively to meet me. I found streets,—
you had just walked down them,
and sometimes in the merchants' shops the mirrors
were still reeling from you and gave back with a start
my too-sudden image. —Who knows if the same
bird did not ring through both of us
yesterday, alone, at evening?

Paris, winter 1913–14

Siehe das leichte Insekt, wie es spielt, nie entriet es
dem geborgenen Schooß.
Die es, entworfen, empfing, trug es aus und erträgts
die Natur, und im gleichen
Mutter-Raum treibt es und west
seine innige Zeit, hüpfend im freudigen
Leib wie der kleine Johannes.
Schon das säugende Tier im erweiterten Aug
staunt

See the carefree insect, how it plays, its whole world
the sheltering womb.
Nature, when it was sketched, received it, bore it,
and bears it now—, and in that same
motherspace it lives and spends
its intimate time, frisking in the joyful
body like a small Saint John.
Whereas the mammal even as it suckles stares
all eye

Paris, early summer 1914

WENDUNG

Der Weg von der Innigkeit zur Größe
geht durch das Opfer.—Kassner

Lange errang ers im Anschaun.
Sterne brachen ins Knie
unter dem ringenden Aufblick.
Oder er anschaute knieend,
und seines Instands Duft
machte ein Göttliches müd,
daß es ihm lächelte schlafend.

Türme schaute er so,
daß sie erschraken:
wieder sie bauend, hinan, plötzlich, in Einem!
Aber wie oft, die vom Tag
überladene Landschaft
ruhete hin in sein stilles Gewahren, abends.

Tiere traten getrost
in den offenen Blick, weidende,
und die gefangenen Löwen
starrten hinein wie in unbegreifliche Freiheit;
Vögel durchflogen ihn grad,
den gemütigen; Blumen
wiederschauten in ihn
groß wie in Kinder.

Und das Gerücht, daß ein Schauender sei,
rührte die minder,
fraglicher Sichtbaren,
rührte die Frauen.

Schauend wie lang?
Seit wie lange schon innig entbehrend,
flehend im Grunde des Blicks?

TURNING

The path from inner intensity to greatness
leads through sacrifice.—Kassner

He had long won it through gazing.
Stars fell to their knees
under his grappling up-glance.
Or he gazed beseechingly,
and the scent of his urgency
wearied an Immortal,
until it smiled on him from sleep.

Towers he gazed at with such force
that they were startled:
building them up again, abruptly, all in an instant!
But how often the landscape,
overburdened by the day,
rested in his quiet perceiving, at twilight.

Animals stepped trustingly
into his open gaze as they pastured,
and the caged lions
stared in, as into unthinkable freedom;
birds flew straight through it,
as it made room; flowers
gazed back in it
greatly, as in children.

And the rumor that a *gazer* existed
stirred the less clearly,
more questionably visible ones,
stirred women.

Gazing how long?
How long inwardly lacking,
imploring deep down in his glance?

Wenn er, ein Wartender, saß in der Fremde; des Gasthofs
zerstreutes, abgewendetes Zimmer
mürrisch um sich, und im vermiedenen Spiegel
wieder das Zimmer
und später vom quälenden Bett aus
wieder:
da beriets in der Luft,
unfaßbar beriet es
über sein fühlbares Herz,
über sein durch den schmerzhaft verschütteten Körper
dennoch fühlbares Herz
beriet es und richtete:
daß es der Liebe nicht habe.

(Und verwehrte ihm weitere Weihen.)

Denn des Anschauns, siehe, ist eine Grenze.
Und die geschautere Welt
will in der Liebe gedeihn.

Werk des Gesichts ist getan,
tue nun Herz-Werk
an den Bildern in dir, jenen gefangenen; denn du
überwältigtest sie: aber nun kennst du sie nicht.
Siehe, innerer Mann, dein inneres Mädchen,
dieses errungene aus
tausend Naturen, dieses
erst nur errungene, nie
noch geliebte Geschöpf.

When he, forever waiting, sat far from home; the hotel's
distracted, turned-aside room
sullenly around him, and in the avoided mirror
again the room
and later from the tormenting bed
again:
there was counsel in the air,
beyond grasping there was counsel
over his still feelable heart,
over his heart which through the buried-alive body
could nevertheless be felt
they held counsel and passed judgment:
it did not have love.

(And forbade him further consecrations.)

For the act of gazing sets limits.
And the world gazed at more deeply
wants to flourish in love.

Work of the eyes is done,
begin heartwork now
on those images in you, those captive ones;
for you conquered them: but now you don't know them.
Behold, inner man, your inner woman,
she who was won
from a thousand natures, she
the till now only won,
as yet never loved creation.

Paris, June 20, 1914

KLAGE

Wem willst du klagen, Herz? Immer gemiedener
ringt sich dein Weg durch die unbegreiflichen
Menschen. Mehr noch vergebens vielleicht,
da er die Richtung behält,
Richtung zur Zukunft behält,
zu der verlorenen.

Früher. Klagtest? Was wars? Eine gefallene
Beere des Jubels, unreife.
Jetzt aber bricht mir mein Jubel-Baum,
bricht mir im Sturme mein langsamer
Jubel-Baum.
Schönster in meiner unsichtbaren
Landschaft, der du mich kenntlicher
machtest Engeln, unsichtbaren.

LAMENT

To whom, heart, would you lament? Ever more avoided
your path struggles through incomprehensible
humankind. The more in vain perhaps
since it holds to the course,
holds the course toward the future,
toward the lost.

Once before. You lamented? What was it? A fallen
berry of jubilation, unripe.
But now my tree of jubilation breaks,
my slow jubilation tree
breaks in the storm.
Loveliest thing in my invisible
landscape, you that made me more easily seen
by angels, themselves invisible.

Paris, July 1914

›MAN MUSS STERBEN WEIL MAN SIE KENNT‹

*(›Papyrus Prisse‹. Aus den Sprüchen des Ptah-hotep,
Handschrift um 2000 v. Ch.)*

›Man muß sterben weil man sie kennt.‹ Sterben
an der unsäglichen Blüte des Lächelns. Sterben
an ihren leichten Händen. Sterben
an Frauen.

Singe der Jüngling die tödlichen,
wenn sie ihm hoch durch den Herzraum
wandeln. Aus seiner blühenden Brust
sing er sie an:
unerreichbare! Ach, wie sie fremd sind.
Über den Gipfeln
seines Gefühls gehn sie hervor und ergießen
süß verwandelte Nacht ins verlassene
Tal seiner Arme. Es rauscht
Wind ihres Aufgangs im Laub seines Leibes. Es glänzen
seine Bäche dahin.

Aber der Mann
schweige erschütterter. Er, der
pfadlos die Nacht im Gebirg
seiner Gefühle geirrt hat:
schweige.

Wie der Seemann schweigt, der ältere,
und die bestandenen
Schrecken spielen in ihm wie in zitternden Käfigen.

"ONE MUST DIE BECAUSE ONE HAS KNOWN THEM"

*("Papyrus Prisse." From the sayings of Ptah-hotep,
manuscript ca. 2000 B.C.)*

"One must die because one has known them." Die
of their smile's unsayable flower. Die
of their light hands. Die
of women.

Let the youth sing those deadly ones
as they come spiraling up through heartspace.
Out of his burgeoning breast
let him sing to them:
unattainable! Ah, how strange they are.
Over the peaks
of his feeling they rise and pour
sweetly transfigured night into the desolate
vale of his arms. Breeze of their
rising leafs through his body's boughs. Glistening
his brooks run forth.

But may the grown man
keep silent more shakenly. He
who, pathless, at night on his feelings'
far ranges has strayed:
keep silent.

As the sailor keeps silent, the older one,
and the outlasted
terrors play in him as in trembling cages.

Paris, July 1914

Fast wie am Jüngsten Tag die Toten sich reißen
aus der Umarmung der Erde, und der erleichterte Ball
hinter ihnen empor sich in die Himmel verliert—:
so fast stürzen sich jetzt diese, die leben, ins Erdreich,
und die beladene sinkt, die Erde, zum Weltgrund
in der Jahrtausende Tang, wo die Schicksale noch—
stumme mit stumpfem Fischblick—
kalte Begegnungen haben. Wo aus Röhren hervor,
wie See-Anemonen,
prachtvoll die Wunden erblühn, und dem furchtbaren Pulp
selber die Strömung den Tast-Arm
an das zu Fassende trägt. Da bildet
aus dem gebeinernen Kalk sich die blasse Koralle
starrlebendigen Grauns, die sich schweigend verzweigt.

Almost as on the last day the dead will tear themselves
from the earth's embrace, and the unburdened ball,
racing after them, will vanish into the sky—:
thus almost now these, the living, plunge into the soil,
and that soil, the earth, sinks laden toward the watery worldbed
into millennial weed, where destinies as yet—
mutely with blank fishgaze—
have cold encounters. Where out of tubes,
as with sea anemones,
wounds bloom resplendently, and the terrible pulp's
waving slime-arm is borne by the current
toward the thing to be seized. On the floor
out of skeletal lime the pale coral's
stiff-living horror evolves, and branches in silence.

Irschenhausen, early September 1914

AN HÖLDERLIN

Verweilung, auch am Vertrautesten nicht,
ist uns gegeben; aus den erfüllten
Bildern stürzt der Geist zu plötzlich zu füllenden; Seen
sind erst im Ewigen. Hier ist Fallen
das Tüchtigste. Aus dem gekonnten Gefühl
überfallen hinab ins geahndete, weiter.

Dir, du Herrlicher, war, dir war, du Beschwörer, ein ganzes
Leben das dringende Bild, wenn du es aussprachst,
die Zeile schloß sich wie Schicksal, ein Tod war
selbst in der lindesten, und du betratest ihn; aber
der vorgehende Gott führte dich drüben hervor.

O du wandelnder Geist, du wandelndster! Wie sie doch alle
wohnen im warmen Gedicht, häuslich, und lang
bleiben im schmalen Vergleich. Teilnehmende. Du nur
ziehst wie der Mond. Und unten hellt und verdunkelt
deine nächtliche sich, die heilig erschrockene Landschaft,
die du in Abschieden fühlst. Keiner
gab sie erhabener hin, gab sie ans Ganze
heiler zurück, unbedürftiger. So auch
spieltest du heilig durch nicht mehr gerechnete Jahre
mit dem unendlichen Glück, als wär es nicht innen, läge
keinem gehörend im sanften
Rasen der Erde umher, von göttlichen Kindern verlassen.
Ach, was die Höchsten begehren, du legtest es wunschlos
Baustein auf Baustein: es stand. Doch selber sein Umsturz
irrte dich nicht.

Was, da ein solcher, Ewiger, war, mißtraun wir
immer dem Irdischen noch? Statt am Vorläufigen ernst

TO HÖLDERLIN

Lingering, even among what's most intimate,
is not our option. From fulfilled images
the spirit abruptly plunges toward ones to be filled;
there are no lakes until eternity. Here falling
is our best. From the mastered emotion
we fall over into the half-sensed, onward and onward.

For you, you superb one, you conjurer,
the urgent image was an entire life, when you pronounced it
the line locked shut like fate, a death was
even in the mildest one, and you entered it; but
the god ahead led you out and beyond.

O you wandering spirit, deftest at change! How all the others
dwell in warm poems, snugly, and make long stays
in narrow similes. Taking part. Only you
drift like the moon. And down below, your nocturnal
landscape grows bright and darkens—that sacredly startled
landscape you feel in departure. No one ever
gave it up more sublimely, gave it back to the whole
more uninjured, less marred by need. So too,
during years you'd ceased counting, you played devoutly
with that infinite happiness, as though it were not inside you
but lay all about, belonging to no one, in the earth's
soft grasses, left there by celestial children.
Ah, what the highest crave, you, undesiring, erected
brick on brick: it stood. Even its collapse
left you unbewildered.

Why, after such a life, Eternal, do we go on
mistrusting the earthly? Instead of from provisional things

die Gefühle zu lernen für welche
Neigung, künftig im Raum?

ardently learning the feelings for who knows
what inclination, awaiting us in space?

Irschenhausen, September 1914

Ausgesetzt auf den Bergen des Herzens. Siehe, wie klein dort,
siehe: die letzte Ortschaft der Worte, und höher,
aber wie klein auch, noch ein letztes
Gehöft von Gefühl. Erkennst du's?
Ausgesetzt auf den Bergen des Herzens. Steingrund
unter den Händen. Hier blüht wohl
einiges auf; aus stummem Absturz
blüht ein unwissendes Kraut singend hervor.
Aber der Wissende? Ach, der zu wissen begann
und schweigt nun, ausgesetzt auf den Bergen des Herzens.
Da geht wohl, heilen Bewußtseins,
manches umher, manches gesicherte Bergtier,
wechselt und weilt. Und der große geborgene Vogel
kreist um der Gipfel reine Verweigerung.—Aber
ungeborgen, hier auf den Bergen des Herzens. . . .

On the mountains of the heart cast out to die. Look, how small there,
 look: the last village of words, and higher,
but how small too, yet one last
farmstead of feeling. Do you see it?
On the mountains of the heart cast out to die. Rockground
under the hands. Here, it's true,
some things flourish; out of mute downplunge
an unknowing herb breaks forth singing.
But for the one who knows? Ah, who began to know
and now is silent, on the mountains of the heart left to die.
True, many an unhurt consciousness roams here,
many, so many sure mountain animals
change fields and stay. And the great sheltered bird
circles the peaks' pure refusal. —But
unsheltered, here on the mountains of the heart . . .

Irschenhausen, September 20, 1914

Immer wieder, ob wir der Liebe Landschaft auch kennen
und den kleinen Kirchhof mit seinen klagenden Namen
und die furchtbar verschweigende Schlucht, in welcher die andern
enden: immer wieder gehn wir zu zweien hinaus
unter die alten Bäume, lagern uns immer wieder
zwischen die Blumen, gegenüber dem Himmel.

Again and again, even though we know love's landscape
and the little churchyard with its lamenting names
and the terrible reticent gorge in which the others
end: again and again the two of us go out together
under the ancient trees, lay ourselves down again and again
among the flowers, facing opposite the sky.

Munich (?), end of 1914

Ach wehe, meine Mutter reißt mich ein.
Da hab ich Stein auf Stein zu mir gelegt,
und stand schon wie ein kleines Haus, um das sich groß der Tag
      bewegt,
sogar allein.
Nun kommt die Mutter, kommt und reißt mich ein.

Sie reißt mich ein, indem sie kommt und schaut.
Sie sieht es nicht, daß einer baut.
Sie geht mir mitten durch die Wand von Stein.
Ach wehe, meine Mutter reißt mich ein.

Die Vögel fliegen leichter um mich her.
Die fremden Hunde wissen: das ist *der*.
Nur einzig meine Mutter kennt es nicht,
mein langsam mehr gewordenes Gesicht.

Von ihr zu mir war nie ein warmer Wind.
Sie lebt nicht dorten, wo die Lüfte sind.
Sie liegt in einem hohen Herz-Verschlag
und Christus kommt und wäscht sie jeden Tag.

Ah misery, my mother tears me down.
I had fitted stone on stone to make me
and stood already like a small house around which the day
    moves spaciously,
even all alone.
Now Mother comes, comes and tears me down.

Simply her coming and looking is enough.
She doesn't see that someone builds.
She walks straight through my walls of stone.
Ah misery, my mother tears me down.

The birds circle me in lighter flight.
The strange dogs know: it's *him*.
Only my mother doesn't recognize it—
my painstakingly fashioned face.

No warm wind ever blew from her to me.
She doesn't live where the breezes stir.
She lies high in a cramped heart-hutch
And Christ comes and washes her each day.

Munich, October 1915

DER TOD MOSES

Keiner, der finstere nur gefallene Engel
wollte; nahm Waffen, trat tödlich
den Gebotenen an. Aber schon wieder
klirrte er hin rückwärts, aufwärts,
schrie in die Himmel: Ich kann nicht!

Denn gelassen durch die dickichte Braue
hatte ihn Moses gewahrt und weitergeschrieben:
Worte des Segens und den unendlichen Namen.
Und sein Auge war rein bis zum Grunde der Kräfte.

Also der Herr, mitreißend die Hälfte der Himmel,
drang herab und bettete selber den Berg auf;
legte den Alten. Aus der geordneten Wohnung
rief er die Seele; die, auf! und erzählte
vieles Gemeinsame, eine unzählige Freundschaft.

Aber am Ende wars ihr genug. Daß es genug sei,
gab die vollendete zu. Da beugte der alte
Gott zu dem Alten langsam sein altes
Antlitz. Nahm ihn im Kusse aus ihm
in sein Alter, das ältere. Und mit Händen der Schöpfung
grub er den Berg zu. Daß es nur einer,
ein wiedergeschaffener, sei unter den Bergen der Erde,
Menschen nicht kenntlich.

THE DEATH OF MOSES

None of them, only the dark, fallen angel
was willing; took weapons, stepped with deadly aim
toward the commanded one. But already
he was clanging backwards, upwards,
and shouting into the heavens: I can't!

For calmly through his brow's thicket
Moses had noticed him and continued writing:
words of blessing and the infinite name.
And his eye was pure to the very depth of his powers.

So the Lord, tearing half the heavens with him,
forced his way down and prepared the mountainbed himself;
laid the old man on it. From her ordered dwelling
he called the soul; up she sped, and recounted
so many things in common, an unsummable friendship.

But in the end she was satisfied. Fulfilled, she
admitted it was time. Then the old god
slowly bowed his old countenance
to the old man. With a kiss extracted him
into his own older age. And with hands of creation
closed up the mountaintomb. So that it would be merely one,
a re-created one, among the mountains of the earth,
indistinguishable to men.

Lines 1–14, Paris, summer 1914; lines 15–22, Munich, October 1915

DER TOD

Da steht der Tod, ein bläulicher Absud
in einer Tasse ohne Untersatz.
Ein wunderlicher Platz für eine Tasse:
steht auf dem Rücken einer Hand. Ganz gut
erkennt man noch an dem glasierten Schwung
den Bruch des Henkels. Staubig. Und: ›*Hoff-nung*‹
an ihrem Bug in aufgebrauchter Schrift.

Das hat der Trinker, den der Trank betrifft,
bei einem fernen Frühstück ab-gelesen.

Was sind denn das für Wesen,
die man zuletzt wegschrecken muß mit Gift?

Blieben sie sonst? Sind sie denn hier vernarrt
in dieses Essen voller Hindernis?
Man muß ihnen die harte Gegenwart
ausnehmen, wie ein künstliches Gebiß.
Dann lallen sie. Gelall, Gelall. . . .
. . . .

O Sternenfall,
von einer Brücke einmal eingesehn—:
Dich nicht vergessen. Stehn!

DEATH

And here we have Death, a bluish distillate
in a cup without a saucer.
A peculiar place for a cup:
set on the back of a hand. One can still see
clearly the break of the handle
on the glazed slope. Dusty. And around its edge
"Hope" fractured in worn-out writing.

That's what the drinker whom the drink was for
at a distant morning meal spelled out.

What sort of beings are these, then,
who finally must be frightened off with poison?

Would they remain otherwise? Are they so engrossed here
in this meal full of hindrance?
This hard present moment has to be pulled out
of them like a set of false teeth.
Then their tongues babble. Lal, gelall. . . .
. . . .

O fall of stars,
glimpsed once from the vantage of a bridge—:
Never to forget you. To stay!

Munich, November 9, 1915

DIE WORTE DES HERRN
AN JOHANNES AUF PATMOS

Siehe: (denn kein Baum soll dich zerstreuen)
reinen Raum auf diesem Eiland stehn.
Vögel? Sei gefaßt auf Leuen
welche durch die Lüfte gehn.
Bäume würden scheuen,
und ich will nicht, daß sie sehn.

Aber du, du sieh, gewahre, sei
schauender als je ein Mann gewesen.
Du sollst fassen, nehmen, lesen,
schlingen sollst du, die ich dir entzwei
breche, meines Himmels volle Frucht.
Daß der Saft dir in die Augen tropfe,
sollst du knien mit erhobnem Kopfe:
dazu hab ich dich gesucht.

Und sollst schreiben, ohne hin zu sehn;
denn auch dieses ist von Nöten: schreibe.
Leg die Rechte rechts und links auf den
Stein die Linke: daß ich beide treibe.

Und nun will ich ganz geschehn.

Jahrmillionen muß ich mich verhalten,
weil die Welten langsamer verleben,
muß den kalten
nach und nach von meinen Gluten geben
statt in allen, alle Glut zu sein.
Und so bin ich niemals im Geschaffnen:

THE WORDS OF THE LORD
TO JOHN ON PATMOS

Behold: (for no tree shall distract you)
pure space stands on this island.
Birds? Be prepared for lions
than run rampant through the air.
Trees would be frightened,
and I choose not to have them see.

But *you, you* shall see, shall perceive, shall
gaze more deeply than anyone before.
You shall seize, take, read,
shall gulp what I split apart for you,
my heaven's ripe fruit.
You shall kneel with upturned head
so that the juice may run into your eyes:
it's why I've sought you out.

And you shall write without looking down:
for that too is why you're here: for writing.
Place your left hand on the stone's left
and your right one on its right: so I can use them both.

And now I'll utterly unfold.

For millions of years I must restrain myself
since worlds take such time evolving,
must pierce their coldness with my ardor
bit by bit, instead of growing fire
in all of them, one giant flame.
And so I'm never wholly in creation:

wenn die Menschen eben mich vermuten,
so vergißt mich schon der Stein.

Einmal will ich mich vor dir entwaffnen.
Meine Mäntel, meine Reichsgewänder,
meine Rüstung: alles, was mich schnürt,
abtun, und dem hohen Doppelhänder
den der Engel für mich führt
meiner Rechten Strom entziehn. Doch jetzt
siehe die Bedeutung meiner Trachten.
Da Wir uns so große Kleider machten,
kommt das Unbekleidetsein zuletzt.

Knechte hat der Satan, die mit Knütteln
niederschlagen, was am zärtsten wächst,
und so muß ich Menschen noch zunächst
in dem eingesehnen Bild bestärken;
doch ich will an meinen Tieren rütteln:
denn es ist ein Drang in meinen Werken,
der nach wachsender Verwandlung lechzt.

Menschen heften sich an die Begriffe,
fanden mühsam sich hinein.
Eine Zeit noch sollen Schiffe Schiffe
und ein Haus soll wie die Häuser sein.
Und der Stuhl, der Tisch, der Schrank, die Truhe
und der Hut, der Mantel und die Schuhe
ohne daß man ihnen etwas tue—:
aber diese Formen sind nicht mein.

Manchmal wenn sie heulen daß ich tobe
werf ich liebend meine Feuerprobe
über das besitzende Geschlecht.
Und ich koste eines ihrer Dinge,

when humans have just started to conjecture me,
I've long been forgotten by the stone.

This once I shall divest myself before you.
My robes, my royal attire,
my armor: all that straps me in
I shall cast off, and from the high great sword
that the angel bears before me shall
withdraw my right hand's force. Yet now
behold the meaning of my garb.
Since we've made ourselves such splendid garments,
stripping-bare awaits us at the end.

Satan has knaves who with cudgels
beat down whatever grows most tenderly,
so for a while yet I must uphold
humans in the clearly outlined image;
but I will set off tremors in my animals:
for there is a thirsting in my works
that craves ever-greater transformation.

Humans work themselves into the concepts
they so laboriously evolved.
For a time yet ships shall be ships
and houses houses.
And chair, table, cupboard, chest
and hat, coat and shoe—
all shall stay as they are;
but these forms are none of mine.

Sometimes when they howl that I'm incensed
I'll cast lovingly my trial of fire
over that complacently possessive race.
And I'll taste one of their things,

ob ich es empfinge——:
wenn es aufbrennt ist es echt.

Wüßten Menschen was der Engel Seele
hinreißt, daß sie wie ein Katarakt
über meine ältesten Befehle
weiterstürzt——. Ich hätte die Kameele
längst zurückgenommen und zerhackt.
An der Bildung ist mir nichts gelegen
denn ich bin der Feuerregen
und mein Blick ist, wie der Blitz gezackt.

Sieh ich dulde nicht daß einer bleibe.
Schreibe:
denn durch ihres Leibes Staub
werfe ich die Männer nach der Scheibe
nach dem Werke oder nach dem Weibe
und die Weiber will ich, wie das Laub.
Nur im Kinde mach ich eine Pause
daß sich das verbreitete Gebrause
sammele im muscheligen Ohr.
Sieh, in diesem Engen, Hingestellten
ordn ich das Gewühle meiner Welten:
das Vergehende geht in ihm vor.

to see if I'd like it——:
if it catches fire it's real.

If humans only knew what transports
an angel's soul, so that like a cataract
it plunges wildly over my oldest
commandments——. I should have long ago
taken back camels and hacked them to pieces.
Form-nurturing is no concern of mine
for I am the rain of fire
and my glance is jagged like the lightning.

I'll not suffer one human to *remain*.
Write:
given their bodies' dust
I turn men out as on a potter's wheel
in the workman's fashion or after woman's way
and I'll have these women as the leaves.
Only in the child sometimes I pause
so that the far-flung outroar
may gather in its conchlike ear.
Behold, within this one small place
I put in order the tumult of my worlds:
in it the perishing proceeds.

Munich, late November 1915

Kreuzweg des Leibes. Und sind doch die himmlischen Straßen
welche uns bilden: den Platz, wo es trübe weht.
Maßlos kommen sie an und sind ohne Maßen
hinaus in den reinen Raum gedreht.

The body's crossroads: and yet the heavenly streets
that make us what we are: bleakly gusting city-square.
They come striding in and with equal swiftness
are turned round and out into pure space.

Spring or summer 1916

Da wird der Hirsch zum Erdteil. Hebt und trägt
den Winterbaum, sein reines unbelaubtes
verzweigtes Spiel. Der Friede seines Hauptes
reicht nicht soweit, daß er in Blätter schlägt.

Now the stag becomes part of earth. Lifts and holds
the tree of winter, its pure unfoliated
branched-out play. The peacefulness of its head
stops just short of breaking into leaves.

Munich, September–October 1916

Graue Liebesschlangen hab ich aus deinen
Achselhöhlen gescheucht. Wie auf heißen Steinen
liegen sie jetzt auf mir und verdauen
Lust-Klumpen

Gray love-snakes I have startled
out of your armpits. As on hot stones
they lie on me now and digest
lumps of lust

Munich, probably 1915 or 1916

Nur zu Verlierern spricht das Verwandelte. Alle Haltenden würgen.

The transformed speaks only to relinquishers. All holders-on are stranglers.

Böckel, early autumn 1917

Musik: Atem der Statuen. Vielleicht:
Stille der Bilder. Du Sprache wo Sprachen
enden. Du Zeit,
die senkrecht steht auf der Richtung vergehender Herzen.

Gefühle zu wem? O du der Gefühle
Wandlung in was?—: in hörbare Landschaft.
Du Fremde: Musik. Du uns entwachsener
Herzraum. Innigstes unser,
das, uns übersteigend, hinausdrängt,—
heiliger Abschied:
da uns das Innre umsteht
als geübteste Ferne, als andre
Seite der Luft:
rein,
riesig,
nicht mehr bewohnbar.

TO MUSIC

Music: breathing of statues. Perhaps:
stillness of paintings. You language where languages
end. You time,
placed erect on the course of hearts that expire.

Feelings . . . for whom? O you the mutation
of feelings . . . into what?—: into audible landscape.
You stranger: music. You heartspace
grown up from us. Innermost thing of ours,
which, exceeding us, crowds out,—
sacred farewell:
when the inner surrounds us
as the most practiced distance, as the air's
other side:
pure,
gigantic,
no longer to be lived in.

Munich, January 11–12, 1918

Gott läßt sich nicht wie leichter Morgen leben.
Wer einfährt in den Schacht, der hat der vollen
Erde Gefühl um Werkschaft aufzugeben:
der steht gebückt und lockert ihn im Stollen.

God won't be lived like some light morning.
Whoever climbs down the shaft must give up
earth's repleteness for the craft of mining:
stand hunched and pry him loose in tunnels.

Munich, mid-March 1919

Die Puppe. *Versuchung!*
Die geladene Puppe, die in den Abgrund fällt

The Doll. *Temptation!*
The loaded doll, which falls into the chasm

Schloss Berg am Irchel, December 1920

Dies überstanden haben: auch das Glück
freudig bestanden haben, still und gründlich.
Bald war die Prüfung stumm, bald war sie mündlich.
Wer schaute nicht verwundert her zurück?

Gekonnt hats keiner, denn das Leben währt,
weils keiner konnte.—Aber der Versuche
Unendlichkeit. Das neue Grün der Buche
ist nicht so neu, wie was uns widerfährt.

Waldtaube gurrt. Und wieder scheint dir ach
was du erlittest, wie noch unerlitten.
Der Vogel ruft. Du bist inmitten
des Vogelrufs. Zugleich erwacht und schwach.

To have come through it: to have joyfully
survived even the happiness—quietly, completely.
First the testings were mute, then verbal.
Who could look back unamazed?

No one has *been able*, since life lasts
because no one *could.* —But the infiniteness
of the attempts! The new greenness of birch trees
is not so new as that which befalls us.

A wood dove coos. And again what you suffered
seems, ah, as if yet unlived-through.
The bird keeps calling. You are in the middle
of the call. Awake and weakened.

Schloss Berg am Irchel, beginning of April 1921

DIE HAND

Siehe die kleine Meise,
hereinverirrte ins Zimmer:
zwanzig Herzschläge lang
lag sie in einer Hand.
Menschenhand. Einer zu schützen entschlossenen.
Unbesitzend beschützenden.
Aber
jetzt auf dem Fensterbrett
frei
bleibt sie noch immer im Schrecken
sich selber
und dem Umgebenden fremd,
dem Weltall, erkennts nicht.
Ach so beirrend ist Hand
selbst noch im Retten.
In der beiständigsten Hand
ist noch Todes genug
und war Geld

THE HAND

See the little titmouse,
lost and bewildered in the room:
twenty heartbeats long
it lay in a hand.
Human hand. One determined to protect.
Unpossessingly protect.
But
now on the windowsill
free
it remains cut off in its fear
from itself
and what surrounds it,
the cosmos, which it doesn't recognize.
Ah, how perplexing a hand is
even bent on rescue.
Even the most assistance-giving hand
still has death enough
and held money

Muzot, end of 1921

Solang du Selbstgeworfnes fängst, ist alles
Geschicklichkeit und läßlicher Gewinn—;
erst wenn du plötzlich Fänger wirst des Balles,
den eine ewige Mit-Spielerin
dir zuwarf, deiner Mitte, in genau
gekonntem Schwung, in einem jener Bögen
aus Gottes großem Brücken-Bau:
erst dann ist Fangen-Können ein Vermögen,—
nicht deines, einer Welt. Und wenn du gar
zurückzuwerfen Kraft und Mut besäßest,
nein, wunderbarer: Mut und Kraft vergäßest
und schon geworfen *hättest* . . . . . (wie das Jahr
die Vögel wirft, die Wandervogelschwärme,
die eine ältre einer jungen Wärme
hinüberschleudert über Meere—) erst
in diesem Wagnis spielst du gültig mit.
Erleichterst dir den Wurf nicht mehr; erschwerst
dir ihn nicht mehr. Aus deinen Händen tritt
das Meteor und rast in seine Räume . . .

As long as you catch self-thrown things
it's all dexterity and venial gain—;
only when you've suddenly caught that ball
which she, one of the eternal players,
has tossed toward you, your center, with
a throw precisely judged, one of those arches
that exist in God's great bridge-system:
only then is catching a proficiency,—
not yours, a world's. And if you then had
strength and courage to return the throw,
no, more wonderful: forgot strength and courage
and had *already* thrown . . . . . (as the year
throws the birds, those migrating bird swarms,
which an older to a younger warmth sends
catapulting across oceans—) only
in that venture would you truly join in.
No longer making the throw easy; no longer making
it hard. Out of your hands the meteor
would launch itself and flame into its spaces . . .

Muzot, January 31, 1922

. . . Wann wird, wann wird, wann wird es genügen
das Klagen und Sagen? Waren nicht Meister im Fügen
menschlicher Worte gekommen? Warum die neuen Versuche?

Sind nicht, sind nicht, sind nicht vom Buche
die Menschen geschlagen wie von fortwährender Glocke?
Wenn dir, zwischen zwei Büchern, schweigender Himmel
      erscheint: frohlocke . . . ,
oder ein Ausschnitt einfacher Erde im Abend.

Mehr als die Stürme, mehr als die Meere haben
die Menschen geschrieen . . . Welche Übergewichte von Stille
müssen im Weltraum wohnen, da uns die Grille
hörbar blieb, uns schreienden Menschen. Da uns die Sterne
schweigende scheinen, im angeschrieenen Äther!

Redeten uns die fernsten, die alten und ältesten Väter!
Und wir: Hörende endlich! Die ersten hörenden Menschen.

. . . When will, when will, when will it be enough,
the saying and lamenting? Have not master formulators
of human words been here? Why the new attempts?

Are not, are not, are not humans
hammered at by books as by perpetual bells?
When, between two books, silent sky appears: rejoice . . . ,
or simply a patch of earth at evening.

Louder than storms, louder than oceans, humans
have been crying out . . . What preponderance of quietness
must abide in cosmic space, since the cricket
remains audible to us, for all our screaming. When the star
shines silently for us, in the screamed-at ether!

If the remotest, the old and most ancient fathers would talk
        to us!
And we: listeners at last! The first human listeners.

Muzot, February 1, 1922

GEGEN-STROPHEN

Oh, daß ihr hier, Frauen, einhergeht,
hier unter uns, leidvoll,
nicht geschonter als wir und dennoch imstande,
selig zu machen wie Selige.

Woher,
wenn der Geliebte erscheint,
nehmt ihr die Zukunft?
Mehr, als je sein wird.
Wer die Entfernungen weiß
bis zum äußersten Fixstern,
staunt, wenn er diesen gewahrt,
euern herrlichen Herzraum.
Wie, im Gedräng, spart ihr ihn aus?
Ihr, voll Quellen und Nacht.

Seid ihr wirklich die gleichen,
die, da ihr Kind wart,
unwirsch im Schulgang
anstieß der ältere Bruder?
Ihr Heilen.

Wo wir als Kinder uns schon
häßlich für immer verzerrn,
wart ihr wie Brot vor der Wandlung.

Abbruch der Kindheit
war euch nicht Schaden. Auf einmal
standet ihr da, wie im Gott
plötzlich zum Wunder ergänzt.

Wir, wie gebrochen vom Berg,
oft schon als Knaben scharf
an den Rändern, vielleicht

ANTISTROPHES

Ah, women, that you are here on earth, that you
move here among us, grief-filled,
no more watched over than we and yet able
to bless like the blessed.

From what region,
when the loved one appears,
do you take the future?
More than will ever exist.
He who knows distances
out to the outermost fixed star
is amazed to find this,
your magnificent heartspace.
How, in the crush, do you keep it free?
You, full of sources and night.

Are you really the same
as those girls who on the path
to school were rudely
shoved aside by an older brother?
You whole ones.

Whereas we, even when children, hatefully
disfigure ourselves forever,
you were like bread before the Change.

Childhood's breaking-off
did you no harm. All at once
you stood there, complete,
as if made manifest in the god.

We, as if broken from cliffs,
even as young boys sharp
at the edges, though sometimes

manchmal glücklich behaun;
wir, wie Stücke Gesteins,
über Blumen gestürzt.

Blumen des tieferen Erdreichs,
von allen Wurzeln geliebte,
ihr, der Eurydike Schwestern,
immer voll heiliger Umkehr
hinter dem steigenden Mann.

Wir, von uns selber gekränkt,
Kränkende gern und gern
Wiedergekränkte aus Not.
Wir, wie Waffen, dem Zorn
neben den Schlaf gelegt.

Ihr, die ihr beinah Schutz seid, wo niemand
schützt. Wie ein schattiger Schlafbaum
ist der Gedanke an euch
für die Schwärme des Einsamen.

perhaps smoothly cut;
we, like large chunks of stone
dumped over flowers.

Flowers of the deeper soil,
loved by all roots,
you, Eurydice's sisters,
always full of sacred turning-back
behind the ascending man.

We, hurt by ourselves, keen
to be hurters and keen
to be hurt back deep inside.
We, like weapons laid
beside anger asleep.

You, who are almost protection where no one
protects. The thought of you
is like a shady sleeptree
for the swarms of the solitary man.

Lines 1–4, Venice, summer 1912; lines 5–46, Muzot, February 9, 1922

Wir, in den ringenden Nächten,
wir fallen von Nähe zu Nähe;
und wo die Liebende taut,
sind wir ein stürzender Stein.

We, in the grappling nights,
we fall from nearness to nearness;
and where the woman in love sweetly thaws,
we are a plunging stone.

Muzot, February 9, 1922

Mein scheuer Mondschatten spräche gern
mit meinem Sonnenschatten von fern
in der Sprache der Toren;
mitten drin ich, ein beschienener Sphinx,
Stille stiftend, nach rechts und links
hab ich die beiden geboren.

My shy moonshadow would like to speak
with my sunshadow from far away
in the language of fools;
I in between, an illumined sphinx,
conferring silence, to the right and left
I've given birth to both.

Muzot, mid-February 1922

VASEN-BILD
(Toten-Mahl)

Sieh, wie unsre Schalen sich durchdringen
ohne Klirrn. Und Wein geht durch den Wein
wie der Mond durch seinen Widerschein
im Gewölk. Oh stilles Weltverbringen . . .
Und der leichte Nicht-Klang spielt wie ein
Schmetterling mit andern Schmetterlingen,
welche tanzen um den warmen Stein.

Blinder Bissen wölbt sich ohne Gröbe,
doch, genährt mit nichts wie die Amöbe,
ließ ich, auch wenn ich ihn näher höbe,
jenen Abstand dauern von vorhin;
und das einzige, das mich selbst verschöbe,
ist der Schritt der Tänzerin.

VASE PAINTING
(Banquet of the Dead)

See how our cups penetrate each other
without clinking. And wine goes through wine
like the moon through its reflection
in the clouds. Oh quiet spending of the world . . .
And the delicate not-clink plays
like a butterfly with other butterflies
that dance around a warm stone.

Blind mouthful arcs without coarseness,
though, nourished on nothing like the amoeba,
I'd allow, even if I brought it closer,
its interval to persist unchanged;
and the one thing that might cause me to shift
is the dancer's step.

Muzot, mid-February 1922

ODETTE R. . . .

Tränen, die innigsten, *steigen!*

O wenn ein Leben
völlig stieg und aus Wolken des eigenen Herzleids
niederfällt: so nennen wir Tod diesen Regen.

Aber fühlbarer wird darüber, uns Armen, das dunkle—,
köstlicher wird, uns Reichen, darüber das seltsame Erdreich.

ODETTE R. . . .

Tears, those most intensely felt, *rise!*

O when a life
has fully risen and from the clouds of its own heartgrief
descends: we call that rain Death.

But then, in our want, the dark soil grows closer to us—,
in our riches, the mysterious loam more prized.

Muzot, December 12, 1922

IMAGINÄRER LEBENSLAUF

Erst eine Kindheit, grenzenlos und ohne
Verzicht und Ziel. O unbewußte Lust.
Auf einmal Schrecken, Schranke, Schule, Frohne
und Absturz in Versuchung und Verlust.

Trotz. Der Gebogene wird selber Bieger
und rächt an anderen, daß er erlag.
Geliebt, gefürchtet, Retter, Ringer, Sieger
und Überwinder, Schlag auf Schlag.

Und dann allein im Weiten, Leichten, Kalten.
Doch tief in der errichteten Gestalt
ein Atemholen nach dem Ersten, Alten . . .

Da stürzte Gott aus seinem Hinterhalt.

IMAGINARY CAREER

First a childhood, boundless and without
negation and goal. O unthinking joy.
Suddenly fright, limit, schoolroom, slavery,
and fall into temptation, into loss.

Defiance. The bent now becomes the bender
and seeks revenge on others, makes *them* succumb.
Loved, dreaded, rescuer, wrestler, victor
and vanquisher, role by role.

And then alone in vastness, lightness, cold.
Yet deep in that erected figure
a breathing toward the First, the Ancient . . .

Then God plunged out of his hiding place.

Schöneck, September 15, 1923

TRÄNENKRÜGLEIN

Andere fassen den Wein, andere fassen die Öle
in dem gehöhlten Gewölb, das ihre Wandung umschrieb.
Ich, als ein kleineres Maß, und als schlankestes, höhle
mich einem andern Bedarf, stürzenden Tränen zulieb.

Wein wird reicher, und Öl klärt sich noch weiter im Kruge.
Was mit den Tränen geschieht?—Sie machten mich schwer,
machten mich blinder und machten mich schillern am Buge,
machten mich brüchig zuletzt und machten mich leer.

LACHRYMATORY

Others carry the wine, others carry the oil
in the hollowed vault their partition circumscribed.
I, as a smaller measure, and as the slimmest, hollow myself
for a different need, for the sake of plummeting tears.

Wine grows richer, and oil grows ever clearer in the jug.
What happens with tears? —They made me heavy,
made me blinder and made me iridescent at the edge,
made me brittle finally and made me empty.

Schönęck, September 16, 1923

Wir sind nur Mund. Wer singt das ferne Herz,
das heil inmitten aller Dinge weilt?
Sein großer Schlag ist in uns eingeteilt
in kleine Schläge. Und sein großer Schmerz
ist, wie sein großer Jubel, uns zu groß.
So reißen wir uns immer wieder los
und sind nur Mund. Aber auf einmal bricht
der große Herzschlag heimlich in uns ein,
so daß wir schrein . . .
Und sind dann Wesen, Wandlung und Gesicht.

We're only mouth. Who sings the distant heart
that dwells whole at the core of all things?
Its great pulse is parceled out among us
into tiny beatings. And its great pain
is, like its great jubilation, too much for us.
So again and again we tear ourselves loose
and are only mouth. But all at once
the great heartbeat secretly breaks in on us
so that we scream . . .
and then are being, transformation, visage.

Schöneck, end of September 1923

Schaukel des Herzens. O sichere, an welchem unsichtbaren
Aste befestigt? Wer, wer gab dir den Stoß,
daß du mit mir bis ins Laub schwangst.
Wie nahe war ich den Früchten, köstlichen. Aber nicht Bleiben
ist im Schwunge der Sinn. Nur das Nahesein, nur
am immer zu Hohen plötzlich das mögliche
Nahsein. Nachbarschaften und dann
von unaufhaltsam erschwungener Stelle
wieder verlorner schon, der neue, der Ausblick.
Und jetzt: die befohlene Umkehr
zurück und hinüber hinaus in des Gleichgewichts Arme.
Unten, dazwischen, das Zögern, der irdische Zwang, der
     Durchgang
durch den Willen der Schwere—, vorbei: und es spannt sich die
     Schleuder,
von der Neugier des Herzens beschwert,
in das andere Gegenteil aufwärts.
Wieder wie anders, wie neu! Wie sie sich beide beneiden
an den Enden des Seils, diese Hälften der Lust.
Viertel, nur Viertel . . . denn drüber
bleibt ja der obere Halbkreis, jener der Himmel
unberührt, unbegonnen—, und selbst für den Kühnsten
zu: überschlüg er sich nicht aus verweigertem Weg?
Aber wie sollten wir nicht, da wir nun einmal alles
ihr verdanken, der ganz unvorsehlichen
Stärke des Stoßes, glauben an jenen
größeren Stoß, der uns ins Runde hinaufwirft?
Denn nicht schaukelt von dort, das an unserem Höhepunkt
     abbräch,
uns ein Spiegelbild nur dieser hiesigen Schwünge entgegen,

Heart's swing. O so securely fastened
to what invisible bough? Who, who gave you that push,
so that you swung me up into the leaves?
How close I was to the fruit, delectable. But not-to-remain
is this momentum's essence. Only the closeness, only
to the ever-too-high suddenly the possible
closeness. Proximities—and then
from the irresistibly swung-up-to place
sure to be lost again, the new view, the prospect.
And now: the commanded reverse
back and across, out into equilibrium's arms. Below,
in between, the hesitation, the force of earth, the passage
through the will of gravity—, on past: and the sling pulls taut,
weighted by the curiosity of the heart,
upward into that other opposite.
Again how different, how new! How they envy each other
at the ends of the rope, these halves of delight!
Quarters, only quarters . . . for there above
the upper half-circle remains, that segment of the heavens
undisturbed, unbegun—, and even for the boldest
closed: would he not plunge headfirst from the barred pathway?
But how should we not, since we do owe everything
to it, to the utterly unforeseeable
strength of the push, have faith in that
greater push that flings us up into the round?
For what swings toward us from there is no mere reflection
(*it* would cease at our apex) of these earthly arcs:

nein, wir ergänzen uns einst durch die Spannung im Raum.
Daß wir ihn spannen, das ists. Daß wir ihn zwischen den Enden
der umkehrenden Kraft spannen

no, one day we'll complete ourselves through the tautness in
    space.
To tauten it, *that's* the key. To stretch it taut between the ends
of the rounding, ever-reversing strength

Muzot, November 6, 1923

Spiele die Tode, die einzelnen, rasch und du wirst sie erkennen
wie sie sich schließt die unendliche Strömung der Sterne;

Play the deaths swiftly through, the single ones, and you will
     see—
how it rounds in upon itself, the infinite stream of stars;

Muzot, end of 1923

FÜR MAX PICARD

Da stehen wir mit Spiegeln:
einer dort . . . . . . , und fangen auf,
und einer da, am Ende nicht verständigt;
auffangend aber und das Bild weither
uns zuerkennend, dieses reine Bild
dem andern reichend aus dem Glanz des Spiegels.
Ballspiel für Götter. Spiegelspiel, in dem
vielleicht drei Bälle, vielleicht neun sich kreuzen,
und keiner jemals, seit sich Welt besann,
fiel je daneben. Fänger, die wir sind.
Unsichtbar kommt es durch die Luft, und dennoch,
wie ganz der Spiegel ihm begegnet, diesem
(in ihm nur völlig Ankunft) diesem Bild,
das nur so lang verweilt, bis wir ermessen,
mit wieviel Kraft es weiter will, wohin.

Nur dies. Und dafür war die lange Kindheit,
und Not und Neigung und der tiefe Abschied
war nur für dieses. Aber dieses lohnt.

FOR MAX PICARD

And so we stand with mirrors:
one of us there . . . . . . , and catch,
and one here, with no notice ever given;
yet catching and passing on the image
singling us out far off, this pure image,
to the other, via the mirror's gleam.
Ball-game for gods! Game of mirrors, in which
three balls, perhaps nine, keep crossing,
none of which, since the world grew conscious,
ever fell wide. Catchers that we are.
It comes invisibly through the air, and yet
how utterly the mirror meets it, this
(in it alone absolute arrival) this image
that stays just long enough for us to gauge
with how much force it would go on, to where.

Only this. And for this the long childhood,
and the need, and the inclinations, and the deep farewell—
only for this. But this repays.

Muzot, November 1923

Daß wir nichts verlieren, daß auch die,
die in Ungeduld vernichten wollen,
immer wieder aus dem Ganzen Vollen
schöpfen müssen. Denn auch sie,
die zerstören

That we lose nothing, that even those
who in impatience would destroy
must again and again to the total fullness
have recourse. For even they,
the annihilators

Muzot, mid-December 1923

FÜR HANS CAROSSA

Auch noch Verlieren ist *unser;* und selbst das Vergessen
hat noch Gestalt in dem bleibenden Reich der Verwandlung.
Losgelassenes kreist; und sind wir auch selten die Mitte
einem der Kreise: sie ziehn um uns die heile Figur.

FOR HANS CAROSSA

Losing also is *ours;* and even forgetting
has a shape in the permanent realm of mutation.
Things we've let go of circle; and though we are rarely a center
of these circles: they trace around us the unbroken figure.

Muzot, February 7, 1924

DER MAGIER

Er ruft es an. Es schrickt zusamm und steht.
Was steht? Das Andre; alles, was nicht er ist,
wird Wesen. Und das ganze Wesen dreht
ein raschgemachtes Antlitz her, das mehr ist.

Oh Magier, halt aus, halt aus, halt aus!
Schaff Gleichgewicht. Steh ruhig auf der Waage,
damit sie einerseits dich und das Haus
und drüben jenes Angewachsne trage.

Entscheidung fällt. Die Bindung stellt sich her.
Er weiß, der Anruf überwog das Weigern.
Doch sein Gesicht, wie mit gedeckten Zeigern,
hat Mitternacht. Gebunden ist auch er.

THE MAGICIAN

He calls it up. It startles into outline.
What's there? The Other; all that he is not
becomes being. And that entire being turns
his way a swiftly fashioned face, that's more.

Oh magician, hold out, hold out, hold out!
Create counterweight. Stand coolly on the scales
that on your side bear you and your house,
and over there that alien accretion.

Decision's reached. The relationship takes hold.
He knows the call outweighed the refusal.
Yet his face, as with dial-hands coinciding,
reads midnight. He's half this spell.

Muzot, February 12, 1924

IRRLICHTER

Wir haben einen alten Verkehr
mit den Lichtern im Moor.
Sie kommen mir wie Großtanten vor . . .
Ich entdecke mehr und mehr

zwischen ihnen und mir den Familienzug,
den keine Gewalt unterdrückt:
diesen Schwung, diesen Sprung, diesen Ruck, diesen Bug,
der den andern nicht glückt.

Auch ich bin dort, wo die Wege nicht gehn,
im Schwaden, den mancher mied,
und ich habe mich oft verlöschen sehn
unter dem Augenlid.

WILL-O'-THE-WISPS

We have an old obscure connection
with the lights on the moor.
They seem to me like great-aunts . . .
More and more I feel

between them and me that family trait
no power can suppress:
this leap, this surge, this jolt, this sudden arc
that the others botch.

I too am there where the paths take detours,
in the vapors most avoided,
and I have often watched myself go out
under my eyelid.

Muzot, mid-February, 1924

Da dich das geflügelte Entzücken
über manchen frühen Abgrund trug,
baue jetzt der unerhörten Brücken
kühn berechenbaren Bug.

Wunder ist nicht nur im unerklärten
Überstehen der Gefahr;
erst in einer klaren reingewährten
Leistung wird das Wunder wunderbar.

Mitzuwirken ist nicht Überhebung
an dem unbeschreiblichen Bezug,
immer inniger wird die Verwebung,
nur Getragensein ist nicht genug.

Deine ausgeübten Kräfte spanne,
bis sie reichen, zwischen zwein
Widersprüchen . . . Denn im Manne
will der Gott beraten sein.

As once the winged energy of delight
carried you over those many first abysses,
now build the unimagined bridge's
sternly calculated arc.

Miracle's not only in the unexplained
outlasting of the threat;
only in the clear, consummate
achievement is the miracle *defined*.

There's no presumption in joining in
on the indescribable relation;
the meshwork grows more and more ardent,
mere being-borne is not enough.

Take your practiced strengths and stretch them
until they reach between two
contradictions . . . For far inside you
the god wishes to consult.

Muzot, mid-February 1924

VORFRÜHLING

Härte schwand. Auf einmal legt sich Schonung
an der Wiesen aufgedecktes Grau.
Kleine Wasser ändern die Betonung.
Zärtlichkeiten, ungenau,

greifen nach der Erde aus dem Raum.
Wege gehen weit ins Land und zeigens.
Unvermutet siehst du seines Steigens
Ausdruck in dem leeren Baum.

EARLY SPRING

Harshness disappeared. Suddenly caring spreads itself
on the field's uncovered gray.
Small rivulets change their intonations.
Tendernesses, inexpertly,

reach toward the earth from space.
Roads run far into the land, foretelling it.
Unexpectedly you see its rising's
visage in the empty tree.

Muzot, mid-February 1924

VERGÄNGLICHKEIT

Flugsand der Stunden. Leise fortwährende Schwindung
auch noch des glücklich gesegneten Baus.
Leben weht immer. Schon ragen ohne Verbindung
die nicht mehr tragenden Säulen heraus.

Aber Verfall: ist er trauriger, als der Fontäne
Rückkehr zum Spiegel, den sie mit Schimmer bestaubt?
Halten wir uns dem Wandel zwischen die Zähne,
daß er uns völlig begreift in sein schauendes Haupt.

TRANSIENCE

Driftsand of hours. Quietly continuous fading
even of the happily blessed building.
Life blows on. Already without connection
the once-supporting columns jut free.

But decline: is it any sadder than the fountain's
turning-back to the mirror, which it dusts with scintilla?
Let us maintain ourselves between change's teeth,
so that its gazing head fully grasps us.

Muzot, end of February 1924

SPAZIERGANG

Schon ist mein Blick am Hügel, dem besonnten,
dem Wege, den ich kaum begann, voran.
So faßt uns das, was wir nicht fassen konnten,
voller Erscheinung, aus der Ferne an—

und wandelt uns, auch wenn wirs nicht erreichen,
in jenes, das wir, kaum es ahnend, sind;
ein Zeichen weht, erwidernd unserm Zeichen . . .
Wir aber spüren nur den Gegenwind.

A WALK

Already my gaze is on the hill, that sunlit one,
up ahead on the path I've scarcely started.
In the same way, what we couldn't grasp grasps us:
blazingly visible, *there* in the distance—

and changes us, even if we don't reach it,
into what we, scarcely sensing it, already are;
a gesture signals, answering our gesture . . .
But we feel only the opposing wind.

Muzot, beginning of March 1924

Weißt du noch: fallende Sterne, die
quer wie Pferde durch die Himmel sprangen
über plötzlich hingehaltne Stangen
unsrer Wünsche—hatten wir so viele?—
denn es sprangen Sterne, ungezählt;
fast ein jeder Aufblick war vermählt
mit dem raschen Wagnis ihrer Spiele,
und das Herz empfand sich als ein Ganzes
unter diesen Trümmern ihres Glanzes
und war heil, als überstünd es sie!

Do you still remember: falling stars, how
they leapt slantwise through the sky
like horses over suddenly held-out hurdles
of our wishes—had we so many?—
for stars, innumerable, leapt everywhere;
almost every look upward was wedded
to the swift hazard of their play,
and the heart felt itself a single thing
beneath that vast disintegration of their brilliance—
and was whole, as though it would survive them!

Muzot, June 1924

WILDER ROSENBUSCH

Wie steht er da vor den Verdunkelungen
des Regenabends, jung und rein;
in seinen Ranken schenkend ausgeschwungen
und doch versunken in sein Rose-sein;

die flachen Blüten, da und dort schon offen,
jegliche ungewollt und ungepflegt:
so, von sich selbst unendlich übertroffen
und unbeschreiblich aus sich selbst erregt,

ruft er dem Wandrer, der in abendlicher
Nachdenklichkeit den Weg vorüberkommt:
Oh sieh mich stehn, sieh her, was bin ich sicher
und unbeschützt und habe was mir frommt.

WILD ROSEBUSH

How it stands out against the darkenings
of the rainy evening, young and pure,
in its tendrils arched everywhere in givingness
and yet absorbed in its rose-being;

the shallow flowers, here and there already open,
each one unasked-for and untended:
thus, immeasurably exceeded by itself
and indescribably self-aroused,

it calls to the wanderer, who in evening
meditation comes past along the road:
Oh look at me, see, over here, how safe I am
and unprotected and having all I need.

Muzot, June 1, 1924

An der sonngewohnten Straße, in dem
hohlen halben Baumstamm, der seit lange
Trog ward, eine Oberfläche Wasser
in sich leis erneuernd, still' ich meinen
Durst: des Wassers Heiterkeit und Herkunft
in mich nehmend durch die Handgelenke.
Trinken schiene mir zu viel, zu deutlich;
aber diese wartende Gebärde
holt mir helles Wasser ins Bewußtsein.

Also, kämst du, braucht ich, mich zu stillen,
nur ein leichtes Anruhn meiner Hände,
sei's an deiner Schulter junge Rundung,
sei es an den Andrang deiner Brüste.

By the sun-accustomed street, in the
hollow half treetrunk which long ago
became a trough, quietly renewing
in itself a shallow water-pool, I still my
thirst; taking in the water's
origin and gladness through my wrists.
Drinking would seem too straightforward, too clear;
but this gesture, more akin to waiting,
fetches bright water into my consciousness.

So that if you came, I'd need, to still myself,
only a light onresting of my hands,—
be it on the young roundness of your shoulders,
be it on the rapture of your breasts.

Muzot, beginning of June 1924

Durch den sich Vögel werfen, ist nicht der
vertraute Raum, der die Gestalt dir steigert.
(Im Freien, dorten, bist du dir verweigert
und schwindest weiter ohne Wiederkehr.)

Raum greift aus uns und übersetzt die Dinge:
daß dir das Dasein eines Baums gelinge,
wirf Innenraum um ihn, aus jenem Raum,
der in dir west. Umgieb ihn mit Verhaltung.
Er grenzt sich nicht. Erst in der Eingestaltung
in dein Verzichten wird er wirklich Baum.

What birds plunge through is not that intimate space
in which you feel all forms intensified.
(There, in the Open, you'd be denied yourself
and vanish on and on without return.)

Space reaches out from us and translates each thing:
to accomplish a tree's essence
cast inner space around it, out of that space
that has its life in you. Surround it with restraint.
In itself it has no bounds. Only in the spell
of your renouncing does it rise as Tree.

Muzot, June 16, 1924

Unstete Waage des Lebens
immer schwankend, wie selten
wagt ein geschicktes Gewicht
anzusagen die immerfort andre
Last gegenüber.

Drüben, die ruhige
Waage des Todes.
Raum auf den beiden
verschwisterten Schalen.
Gleichviel Raum. Und daneben,
ungebraucht,
alle Gewichte des Gleichmuts,
glänzen, geordnet.

Unsteady scales of life
forever swaying, how seldom
a confident weight dares
announce the load of its constantly
altering opposite number.

Across the way, death's
peaceful scales.
Space on the two
brother-and-sister pans.
Distinctionless space. And beside it,
unused,
all of equanimity's weights,
gleaming, in order.

Ragaz, mid-July 1924

Welt war in dem Antlitz der Geliebten—,
aber plötzlich ist sie ausgegossen:
Welt ist draußen, Welt ist nicht zu fassen.

Warum trank ich nicht, da ich es aufhob,
aus dem vollen, dem geliebten Antlitz
Welt, die nah war, duftend meinem Munde?

Ach, ich trank. Wie trank ich unerschöpflich.
Doch auch ich war angefüllt mit zuviel
Welt, und trinkend ging ich selber über.

World was in the face of the beloved—,
but suddenly it was emptied out:
world is outside, world cannot be grasped.

Why didn't I, when I lifted it,
from the full, the cherished face drink
world, which was so near I tasted its bouquet?

Ah, I drank. Insatiably I drank.
But I was filled already with too much
world, and as I drank I overflowed.

Ragaz, mid-July 1924

Ach, im Wind gelöst,
wieviel vergebliche Wiederkehr.
Manches, was uns verstößt,
tut hinterher,
wenn wir vorüber sind,
ratlos die Arme auf.
Denn es giebt keinen Lauf
zurück. Alles hebt uns hinaus,
und das spät offene Haus
bleibt leer.

Ah, adrift in the air,
how much unfulfilled recurrence.
The things that expel us,
so often, afterwards,
once we've gone,
spread hopelessly their arms.
For no course leads back.
Everything lifts us up and across,
and the belatedly open house
remains empty.

Ragaz, mid-July 1924

Eine Furche in meinem Hirn,
eine Linie meiner Hand:
hält die Gewohnheit stand,
wird sie mir beides verwirrn.

Rette dich und entflieh
aus dem verengten Netz.
Wirf ein neues Gesetz
über dich und sie.

A furrow in my brain,
a line etched in my hand:
if habit has its way,
it will confound the two.

Save yourself and flee
the narrowed net.
Cast a new law's circuit
over you and them.

Muzot, early September 1924

HANDINNERES

Innres der Hand. Sohle, die nicht mehr geht
als auf Gefühl. Die sich nach oben hält
und im Spiegel
himmlische Straßen empfängt, die selber
wandelnden.
Die gelernt hat, auf Wasser zu gehn,
wenn sie schöpft,
die auf den Brunnen geht,
aller Wege Verwandlerin.
Die auftritt in anderen Händen,
die ihresgleichen
zur Landschaft macht:
wandert und ankommt in ihnen,
sie anfüllt mit Ankunft.

PALM OF THE HAND

Hand's secret self.   Sole, that has ceased to walk
except on feeling. That holds itself face-up
and in that mirror
receives heavenly streets, themselves
out wandering.
That has learned to walk on water
when it scoops,
that walks on wells,
the alterer of every path it travels.
That appears in other hands,
transforms those like it
into a landscape:
wanders and arrives in them,
fills them with arrival.

Muzot, beginning of October 1924

Nacht. Oh du in Tiefe gelöstes
Gesicht an meinem Gesicht.
Du, meines staunenden Anschauns größtes
Übergewicht.

Nacht, in meinem Blicke erschauernd,
aber in sich so fest;
unerschöpfliche Schöpfung, dauernd
über dem Erdenrest;

voll von jungen Gestirnen, die Feuer
aus der Flucht ihres Saums
schleudern ins lautlose Abenteuer
des Zwischenraums:

wie, durch dein bloßes Dasein, erschein ich,
Übertrefferin, klein—;
doch, mit der dunkelen Erde einig,
wag ich es, in dir zu sein.

Night. Oh you face against my face
dissolved in deepness.
You, my awestruck gaze's vast
preponderance.

Night, in my eyesight shuddering,
but in yourself so firm;
inexhaustible creation, continuing on
over the earth's remains;

full of young starfields that hurl
fire from the black at their edges
into the soundless adventure
of the space-between;

by your very being, transcender,
you make me seem small—;
yet, at one with the dark earth,
I dare exist in you.

Muzot, October 2–3, 1924

SCHWERKRAFT

Mitte, wie du aus allen
dich ziehst, auch noch aus Fliegenden dich
wiedergewinnst, Mitte, du Stärkste.

Stehender: wie ein Trank den Durst
durchstürzt ihn die Schwerkraft.

Doch aus dem Schlafenden fällt,
wie aus lagernder Wolke,
reichlicher Regen der Schwere.

GRAVITY

Center, how you from all things living
extract yourself, even from those that fly win
yourself back, center, you strongest one.

Someone standing: as a drink through thirst
gravity plunges through him.

But from one asleep there falls,
as from a cloud suspended,
gravity's ample rain.

Muzot, October 5, 1924

MAUSOLEUM

Königsherz. Kern eines hohen
Herrscherbaums. Balsamfrucht.
Goldene Herznuß. Urnen-Mohn
mitten im Mittelbau,
(wo der Widerhall abspringt,
wie ein Splitter der Stille,
wenn du dich rührst,
weil es dir scheint,
daß deine vorige
Haltung zu laut war . . .)
Völkern entzogenes,
sterngesinnt,
im unsichtbaren Kreisen
kreisendes Königsherz.

Wo ist, wohin,
jenes der leichten
Lieblingin?
: Lächeln, von außen,
auf die zögernde Rundung
heiterer Früchte gelegt;
oder der Motte, vielleicht,
Kostbarkeit, Florflügel, Fühler . . .

Wo aber, wo, das sie sang,
das sie in Eins sang,
das Dichterherz?
: Wind,
unsichtbar,
Windinnres.

MAUSOLEUM

King's heart. Core of a high
ruler tree. Balsam fruit.
Golden heart nut. Urn poppy
in the middle of the central region
(where the echo cracks off
like a splinter of silence
whenever you stir
because it feels to you
that your previous
position was too loud . . .),
away from nations,
in with stars,
orbiting invisibly
king's heart.

Where is—where vanished—
that of the gentle
girl, his love?
: Smile, from outside,
placed on the hesitant roundness
of happy fruit;
or perhaps the moth's
exquisiteness, gauze wing, feeler . . .

Where, though, that which sang them,
sang them into oneness,
the poet's heart?
: Wind,
invisible,
wind's insideness.

Muʒot, October 1924

Irgendwo blüht die Blume des Abschieds und streut
immerfort Blütenstaub, den wir atmen, herüber;
auch noch im kommendsten Wind atmen wir Abschied.

Somewhere the flower of farewell blooms and scatters
ceaselessly its pollen, which we breathe;
even in the winds that reach us first we breathe farewell.

Muzot, mid-October 1924

Aufgedeckter das Land: auf allen Wegen ist Heimkehr,
durch den gelockerten Baum sieht man das Haus, wie es währt.
Himmel entfernt sich von uns. Wärmt nun, oh Herzen, die Erde,
daß sie uns innig gehört in dem verlassenen Raum.

More unconcealed the land. On every road returnings.
Through the slackened tree one can see the house still waiting
    there.
The sky withdraws from us. Warm now, oh hearts, the earth,
make it all the more deeply ours in forsaken space.

Muzot, end of October 1924

HERBST

Oh hoher Baum des Schauns, der sich entlaubt:
nun heißts gewachsen sein dem Übermaße
von Himmel, das durch seine Äste bricht.
Erfüllt vom Sommer, schien er tief und dicht,
uns beinah denkend, ein vertrautes Haupt.
Nun wird sein ganzes Innere zur Straße
des Himmels. Und der Himmel kennt uns nicht.

Ein Äußerstes: daß wir wie Vogelflug
uns werfen durch das neue Aufgetane,
das uns verleugnet mit dem Recht des Raums,
der nur mit Welten umgeht. Unsres Saums
Wellen-Gefühle suchen nach Bezug
und trösten sich im Offenen als Fahne—
. . . .

Aber ein Heimweh meint das Haupt des Baums.

AUTUMN

Oh gazing's tall tree, shedding leaf on leaf:
now we must face that excess
of sky breaking through its branches.
Fulfilled with summer, it seemed deep and thick,
thinking *us* almost, a sympathetic head.
Now its whole interior is becoming
the sky's street. And the sky doesn't know us.

A last resort: that we as in birdflight
hurl ourselves through this new unfoldedness
that disowns us with the law of space,
which only recognizes worlds. Our margins'
wavefeelings keep seeking for relation
and in the Open find consolation as flags—
. . . .

But a homesickness can't forget that tree.

Muzot, late autumn 1924

O schöner Glanz des scheuen Spiegelbilds!
Wie darf es glänzen, weil es nirgends dauert.
Der Frauen Dürsten nach sich selber stillts.
Wie ist die Welt mit Spiegeln zugemauert

für sie. Wir fallen in der Spiegel Glanz
wie in geheimen Abfluß unseres Wesens;
sie aber finden ihres dort: sie lesens.
Sie müssen doppelt sein, dann sind sie ganz.

Oh, tritt, Geliebte, vor das klare Glas,
auf daß du seist. Daß zwischen dir und dir
die Spannung sich erneue und das Maß
für das, was unaussprechlich ist in ihr.

Gesteigert um dein Bild: wie bist du reich.
Dein Ja zu dir bejaht dir Haar und Wange;
und überfüllt von solchem Selbstempfange,
taumelt dein Blick und dunkelt im Vergleich.

O bright gleam of a shy mirror image!
Gone so quickly, it has full leave to shine.
It stills the thirst women have for themselves.
How the whole world is walled with mirrors

for them. We plunge into the mirror's gleam
as with some occult outpour of our being;
but they find their being there: they read it.
They must be double—then they are whole.

So step, love, before the lucid surface
that you may be. That between yourself and you
that tension may revive, and the measure
for what in you exceeds expression.

Heightened by your image: how rich you are.
Hair and cheek confirm to you your "Yes"
to yourself; brimming from such self-reception,
your gaze reels, and darkens in accord.

Valmont, end of November 1924

... Wenn aus des Kaufmanns Hand
die Waage übergeht
an jenen Engel, der sie in den Himmeln
stillt und beschwichtigt mit des Raumes Ausgleich ...

. . . When from the merchant's hand
the balance passes over
to the angel, who in the heavens
stills and soothes it with space's equanimity . . .

Valmont, end of November 1924

Ach, nicht getrennt sein,
nicht durch so wenig Wandung
ausgeschlossen vom Sternen-Maß.
Innres, was ists?
Wenn nicht gesteigerter Himmel,
durchworfen mit Vögeln und tief
von Winden der Heimkehr.

Ah, not to be cut off,
not by such slight partition
to be excluded from the stars' measure.
What is inwardness?
What if not sky intensified,
flung through with birds and deep
with winds of homecoming?

Paris, summer 1925 (before July 6)

Unaufhaltsam, ich will die Bahn vollenden,
mich schreckt es, wenn mich ein Sterbliches hält.
Einmal hielt mich ein Schooß.
Ihm sich entringen, war tödlich:
ich rang mich ins Leben. Aber sind Arme so tief,
sind sie so fruchtbar, um ihnen
durch die beginnliche Not
neuer Geburt zu entgehn?

Undeterrable, I'll complete this course,
it scares me when something mortal holds me.
Once a womb held me.
To wrestle out of it was deadly:
I wrestled into life. But arms—how deep are arms,
how fertile are they, what chance
that *they* through the inaugural agony
of new birth might be escaped?

Paris, early summer 1925

Jetzt wär es Zeit, daß Götter träten aus
bewohnten Dingen . . .
Und daß sie jede Wand in meinem Haus
umschlügen. Neue Seite. Nur der Wind,
den solches Blatt im Wenden würfe, reichte hin,
die Luft, wie eine Scholle, umzuschaufeln:
ein neues Atemfeld. Oh Götter, Götter!
Ihr Oftgekommnen, Schläfer in den Dingen,
die heiter aufstehn, die sich an den Brunnen,
die wir vermuten, Hals und Antlitz waschen
und die ihr Ausgeruhtsein leicht hinzutun
zu dem, was voll scheint, unserm vollen Leben.
Noch einmal sei es euer Morgen, Götter.
Wir wiederholen. Ihr allein seid Ursprung.
Die Welt steht auf mit euch, und Anfang glänzt
an allen Bruchstelln unseres Mißlingens . . .

Now it is time that gods stepped out
of dwelt-in things . . .
Time they ripped down every wall
in my house. New page. Only the wind
made by such a page turning over
could shovel the air as a spade turns earth:
a new breathfield. Oh gods, gods!
You who came so often, sleepers inside things,
who cheerfully arise, who at wells
which we conjecture wash face and neck
and lightly add your restedness
to that which seems replete, our own full life.
May it once again be your morning, gods.
We repeat. You alone are source.
The world gets up with you, and beginning shines
on all the cracks in our failures . . .

Muʐot, mid-October 1925

Rose, oh reiner Widerspruch, Lust,
Niemandes Schlaf zu sein unter soviel
Lidern.

Rose, O pure contradiction, delight
in being no one's sleep under so many
lids.

Muzot, October 27, 1925

GONG [I]

Klang, nichtmehr mit Gehör
meßbar. Als wäre der Ton,
der uns rings übertrifft,
eine Reife des Raums.

GONG [I]

Sound, no longer measurable
with sense of hearing. As if that tone
outstripping us on every side
were space maturing.

Muzot, end of October 1925

IDOL

Gott oder Göttin des Katzenschlafs,
kostende Gottheit, die in dem dunkeln
Mund reife Augen-Beeren zerdrückt,
süßgewordnen Schauns Traubensaft,
ewiges Licht in der Krypta des Gaumens.
Schlaf-Lied nicht,—Gong! Gong!
Was die anderen Götter beschwört,
entläßt diesen verlisteten Gott
an seine einwärts fallende Macht.

IDOL

God or goddess of the sleep of cats,
savoring deity, who in the dark
mouth crushes ripe eyeberries,
grape juice of seeing grown sweet,
eternal torchlight in the palate's crypt.
Not lullaby, —Gong! Gong!
What conjures all the other gods
lets this god of ancient wiles slip back
into its inwardly receding might.

Line 1, Paris, summer 1925;
lines 2–9, Muzot, November 1925

Nicht mehr für Ohren . . . : Klang,
der, wie ein tieferes Ohr,
uns, scheinbar Hörende, hört.
Umkehr der Räume. Entwurf
innerer Welten im Frein . . . ,
Tempel vor ihrer Geburt,
Lösung, gesättigt mit schwer
löslichen Göttern . . . : Gong!

Summe des Schweigenden, das
sich zu sich selber bekennt,
brausende Einkehr in sich
dessen, das an sich verstummt,
Dauer, aus Ablauf gepreßt,
umgegossener Stern . . . : Gong!

Du, die man niemals vergißt,
die sich gebar im Verlust,
nichtmehr begriffenes Fest,
Wein an unsichtbarem Mund,
Sturm in der Säule, die trägt,
Wanderers Sturz in den Weg,
unser, an Alles, Verrat . . . : Gong!

GONG [II]

No longer for ears . . . : sound
that, like a deeper ear,
hears us, apparent listeners.
Spaces' reversal. Design
for inner worlds out in the Open . . . ,
temple before their birth,
solution, saturated with gods
difficult to dissolve . . . : Gong!

Sum of all things silent, which
confesses to itself alone,
thunderous inturn of something
by itself struck dumb,
duration squeezed from transience,
star re-poured . . . : Gong!

You, whom one never forgets,
who gave birth to yourself in loss,
festival no longer grasped,
wine on invisible lips,
storm in the column which upholds,
wanderer's fall onto the path,
our treason—to everything . . . : Gong!

Muzot, November 1925

Aber versuchtest du dies: Hand in der Hand mir zu sein
wie im Weinglas der Wein Wein ist.
Versuchtest du dies.

But if you'd try this: to be hand in my hand
as in the wineglass the wine is wine.
If you'd try this.

Muzot, end of November 1925

Früher, wie oft, blieben wir, Stern in Stern,
wenn aus dem Sternbild der freiste,
jener Sprech-Stern hervortrat und rief.
Stern in Stern staunten wir,
Er, der Sprecher des Stern-Bilds,
ich, meines Lebens Mund,
Nebenstern meines Augs.
Und die Nacht, wie gewährte sie uns
die durchwachte Verständigung.

Earlier, how often, we'd remain, star in star,
when from the constellation the freest,
the announcing star, stepped forth and called.
Star in star we marveled,
he, the speaker of the star-sign,
I, my life's mouth,
my eye's companion star.
And the night, how it granted us
the wide-awake accord.

Valmont, early February 1926

Die Vogelrufe fangen an zu rühmen.
Und sind im Recht. Wir hören lange hin.
(Wir hinter Masken, ach, und in Kostümen!)
Was rufen sie? ein wenig Eigensinn,

ein wenig Wehmut und sehr viel Versprechen,
das an der halbverschlossnen Zukunft feilt.
Und zwischendurch in unserm Horchen heilt
das schöne Schweigen, das sie brechen.

The birdcalls begin their praise.
And it's their right. We listen closely.
(We behind masks, in costumes!)
What do they call? a little willfulness,

a little sadness, and such huge promise,
sawing away at the half-locked future.
And in between, healing in our hearing:
the beautiful silence that they break.

Valmont, mid-March 1926

Bruder Körper ist arm . . . : da heißt es, reich sein für ihn.
Oft war *er* der Reiche: so sei ihm verziehn
das Armsein seiner argen Momente.
Wenn er dann tut, als ob er uns kaum noch kennte,
darf man ihn leise erinnern an alles Gemeinsame.

Freilich wir sind nicht Eines, sondern zwei Einsame:
unser Bewußtsein und Er;
aber wie vieles, das wir einander weither
verdanken,
wie Freunde es tun! Und man erfährt im Erkranken:
Freunde haben es schwer!

Brother body is poor . . . : then we'll have to be rich for him.
Often *he* was the rich one: so may he be pardoned
the meanness of his worst moments.
If he then acts as though he scarcely still knows us,
let us gently remind him of everything shared.

Granted, we are not one, but a solitary two:
our consciousness and he;
but how much we owe each other
past conceiving,
the way it is with friends! And one learns in illness:
friendship is hard!

Valmont, May 1, 1926

Von nahendem Regen fast zärtlich verdunkelter Garten,
Garten unter der zögernden Hand.
Als besännen sich, ernster, in den Beeten die Arten,
wie es geschah, daß sie ein Gärtner erfand.

Denn sie denken ja ihn; gemischt in die heitere Freiheit
bleibt sein bemühtes Gemüt, bleibt vielleicht sein Verzicht.
Auch an ihnen zerrt, die uns so seltsam erzieht, diese Zweiheit;
noch in dem Leichtesten wecken wir Gegengewicht.

Garden, by approaching rains almost tenderly darkened,
shadowed beneath some hesitating hand.
As if the kinds pondered more deeply in their rows
how a gardener happened to invent them.

For it's of him they think; mixed into their cheerful freedom
his toilsome care remains, perhaps his self-withholding.
They too feel the pull of what so strangely brings us up, this
    splitness;
even in the lightest things we waken counterweight.

Vevey, May 22, 1926

ELEGIE
an Marina Zwetajewa-Efron

O die Verluste ins All, Marina, die stürzenden Sterne!
Wir vermehren es nicht, wohin wir uns werfen, zu welchem
Sterne hinzu! Im Ganzen ist immer schon alles gezählt.
So auch, wer fällt, vermindert die heilige Zahl nicht.
Jeder verzichtende Sturz stürzt in den Ursprung und heilt.
Wäre denn alles ein Spiel, Wechsel des Gleichen, Verschiebung,
nirgends ein Name und kaum irgendwo heimisch Gewinn?
Wellen, Marina, wir Meer! Tiefen, Marina, wir Himmel.
Erde, Marina, wir Erde, wir tausendmal Frühling, wie Lerchen,
die ein ausbrechendes Lied in die Unsichtbarkeit wirft.
Wir beginnens als Jubel, schon übertrifft es uns völlig;
plötzlich, unser Gewicht dreht zur Klage abwärts den Sang.
Aber auch so: Klage? Wäre sie nicht: jüngerer Jubel nach unten.
Auch die unteren Götter wollen gelobt sein, Marina.
So unschuldig sind Götter, sie warten auf Lob wie die Schüler.
Loben, du Liebe, laß uns verschwenden mit Lob.
Nichts gehört uns. Wir legen ein wenig die Hand um die Hälse
ungebrochener Blumen. Ich sah es am Nil in Kôm-Ombo.
So, Marina, die Spende, selber verzichtend, opfern die Könige.
Wie die Engel gehen und die Türen bezeichnen jener zu Rettenden,
also rühren wir dieses und dies, scheinbar Zärtliche, an.
Ach wie weit schon Entrückte, ach, wie Zerstreute, Marina,
auch noch beim innigsten Vorwand. Zeichengeber, sonst nichts.
Dieses leise Geschäft, wo es der Unsrigen einer
nicht mehr erträgt und sich zum Zugriff entschließt,
rächt sich und tötet. Denn daß es tödliche Macht hat,
merkten wir alle an seiner Verhaltung und Zartheit
und an der seltsamen Kraft, die uns aus Lebenden zu
Überlebenden macht. Nicht-Sein. Weißt du's, wie oft
trug uns ein blinder Befehl durch den eisigen Vorraum
neuer Geburt. . . . Trug: *uns?* Einen Körper aus Augen
unter zahllosen Lidern sich weigernd. Trug das in uns
niedergeworfene Herz eines ganzen Geschlechts. An ein Zugvogelziel

ELEGY
to Marina Tsvetayeva-Efron

O the losses into the All, Marina, the falling stars!
We don't augment it, no matter where we fling ourselves, out to
whatever star! In the Whole everything has already
been summed. Nor does one who falls lessen the sacred count.
Each renouncing plunge falls to the source and heals.
Is it all then a game—changing of sameness, displacement,
nowhere a name and scarcely anywhere indigenous gain?
Waves, Marina, we are ocean! Depths, Marina, we are sky!
Earth, Marina, we are earth, are a thousand times spring, like larks
that an outbursting song hurls into the unbeheld.
We commence it as jubilation, from the first it wildly exceeds us;
suddenly our weight bends the song toward lament.
But why "lament"? Why not: "younger jubilation down below"?
Even the gods below want to be praised, Marina.
Gods are so innocent, they await praise like schoolchildren.
Praising, dearest, let us be lavish with praise.
Nothing is ours. We curl our hand lightly around the necks
of unbroken flowers. I saw it on the Nile in Kom Ombo.
In just that way, Marina, kings make the sacrifice a self-withholding.
As angels walk and mark the doors of those to be saved,
we, seemingly tender, touch this one and this.
Ah, how far removed already, how distracted, Marina,
even in our most fervent pretext. Sign-givers, nothing more.
This delicate business, when one of ours loses
patience and tenses himself to clutch,
strikes first and kills. For that it has deadly strength
we could all see in its restraint and tenderness
and in the strange power that turns us from living beings
into survivors. Not-being. Remember how often
a blind command bore us through the icy antechamber
of new birth? . . . Bore *us*? A body of pure eyes
balking beneath myriad eyelids. Bore the hurled-down
heart of an entire race, lodged in us. To a migrating-bird-goal

trug er die Gruppe, das Bild unserer schwebenden Wandlung.
Liebende dürften, Marina, dürfen soviel nicht
von dem Untergang wissen. Müssen wie neu sein.
Erst ihr Grab ist alt, erst ihr Grab besinnt sich, verdunkelt
unter dem schluchzenden Baum, besinnt sich auf Jeher.
Erst ihr Grab bricht ein; sie selber sind biegsam wie Ruten;
was übermäßig sie biegt, ründet sie reichlich zum Kranz.
Wie sie verwehen im Maiwind! Von der Mitte des Immer,
drin du atmest und ahnst, schließt sie der Augenblick aus.
(O wie begreif ich dich, weibliche Blüte am gleichen
unvergänglichen Strauch. Wie streu ich mich stark in die Nachtluft,
die dich nächstens bestreift.) Frühe erlernten die Götter
Hälften zu heucheln. Wir in das Kreisen bezogen
füllten zum Ganzen uns an wie die Scheibe des Monds.
Auch in abnehmender Frist, auch in den Wochen der Wendung
niemand verhülfe uns je wieder zum Vollsein, als der
einsame eigene Gang über der schlaflosen Landschaft.

it bore the group, that image of our vectoring change.
Lovers ought not, Marina, lovers *may* not know
so deeply of decline. Must be as new.
Only their grave ages, only their grave remembers, grows dark
under the sobbing tree, pondering time evermore.
Only their grave caves in; they themselves are supple like reeds;
what bends them violently rounds them richly into wreaths.
How they blow about in the May wind! From the region of Always,
in which you breathe and surmise, the Moment bars them.
(O how I know you, female blossom on the same
undying shrub. How I scatter myself strongly into the nightbreeze
that will soon touch you.) Early on, the gods learned
to simulate halves. We, drawn into the circle,
filled ourselves to the whole like the moon's disk.
Even in the waning phase, even in the weeks of the turning,
no one could ever help us again to fullness—only
our own solitary course over the sleepless landscape.

Muzot, June 8, 1926

VOLLMACHT

Ach entzögen wir uns Zählern und Stundenschlägern.
Einen Morgen hinaus, heißes Jungsein mit Jägern,
    Rufen im Hundegekläff.
Daß im durchdrängten Gebüsch Kühle uns fröhlich besprühe,
und wir im Neuen und Frein—in den Lüften der Frühe
    fühlten den graden Betreff!

Solches war uns bestimmt. Leichte beschwingte Erscheinung.
Nicht, im starren Gelaß, nach einer Nacht voll Verneinung,
    ein verneinender Tag.
Diese sind ewig im Recht: dringend dem Leben Genahte;
weil sie Lebendige sind, tritt das unendlich bejahte
    Tier in den tödlichen Schlag.

FULL POWER

Ah, could we escape counters and strikers of hours.
One morning eagerly outside, hot youthfulness with hunters,
    shouts in the clamor of hounds.
Thrashing through bushes, coolness joyfully spraying us,
and we in the new and the free—feeling in the earliest breezes
    the exact connection.

This we were meant for. Lighthearted exhilarated appearance.
Not, in the rigid room, after a night of negation,
    one more negation-filled day.
These are eternally in the right, these pressed so close to life;
because they are the living, the infinitely affirmed
    animal steps into the mortal blow.

Muzot, June 9, 1926

ANKUNFT

In einer Rose steht dein Bett, Geliebte. Dich selber
(oh ich Schwimmer wider die Strömung des Dufts)
hab ich verloren. So wie dem Leben zuvor
diese (von außen nicht meßbar) dreimal drei Monate sind,
so, nach innen geschlagen, werd ich erst *sein*. Auf einmal,
zwei Jahrtausende vor jenem neuen Geschöpf,
das wir genießen, wenn die Berührung beginnt,
plötzlich: gegen dir über, werd ich im Auge geboren.

ARRIVAL

Inside a rose your bed stands, beloved. You yourself
(oh I the swimmer against the stream of scent)
I have lost. Just as the life before this
has its (from outside not measurable) three times three months,
so, turned at last inward, I shall *be*. All at once,
two millennia before that new creation
which we'll savor when the touching begins,
suddenly: face to face with you, I am born in the eye.

Muzot, June 9, 1926

Komm du, du letzter, den ich anerkenne,
heilloser Schmerz im leiblichen Geweb:
wie ich im Geiste brannte, sieh, ich brenne
in dir; das Holz hat lange widerstrebt,
der Flamme, die du loderst, zuzustimmen,
nun aber nähr' ich dich und brenn in dir.
Mein hiesig Mildsein wird in deinem Grimmen
ein Grimm der Hölle nicht von hier.
Ganz rein, ganz planlos frei von Zukunft stieg
ich auf des Leidens wirren Scheiterhaufen,
so sicher nirgend Künftiges zu kaufen
um dieses Herz, darin der Vorrat schwieg.
Bin ich es noch, der da unkenntlich brennt?
Erinnerungen reiß ich nicht herein.
O Leben, Leben: Draußensein.
Und ich in Lohe. Niemand der mich kennt.

[Verzicht. Das ist nicht so wie Krankheit war
einst in der Kindheit. Aufschub. Vorwand um
größer zu werden. Alles rief und raunte.
Misch nicht in dieses was dich früh erstaunte]

Come, you last thing, which I acknowledge,
unholy agony in the fleshly weave;
just as I burned in spirit, look, I burn
in you; the wood has long held back,
long recoiled from those flames you blaze,
but now I feed you and burn in you.
Inside your rage my native mildness becomes
a raging hell, unlike anything here.
Without plan, completely pure, free of future
I mounted suffering's tangled pyre,
so sure of nowhere buying times to come
for this heart, its store so mute.
Is it still I, burning here beyond recognition?
I will not drag memories inside.
O life, life: externality.
And I in flame. No one knowing me.

[Renunciation. That's not the way illness was
in childhood. Putting-off. Subterfuge
for growing. Everything called and whispered.
Don't mix those early marvels into this]

Valmont, mid-December 1926
Last entry in last pocket-book

Notes

Index of Titles and First Lines in German

Index of Titles and First Lines in English

Notes

page

13 "To Lou Andreas-Salomé." The couple's passionate few years together were more than ten years in an estranged past when this sequence was written. Rilke copied out the three pieces and sent them to Lou along with other poems in a letter of May 18, 1919. The title is an editorial addition.

75 "Head of Amenophis IV in Berlin." Rilke records his encounter with this sculpted Egyptian head in letters to Lou Andreas-Salomé (August 1, 1913) and Princess Marie von Thurn und Taxis-Hohenlohe (August 8, 1913). Some months after writing the poem and the prose description, he elaborates on its significance for him in a letter of February 1, 1914, to Magda von Hattingberg ("Benvenuta"): "When you are in Berlin, go look at the head of Amenophis IV in the central courtyard of the Egyptian Museum . . . , feel, in this face, what it means to be over against the infinite world and, within so limited a surface, through the heightened arrangement of a few features, to form a counterpoise to the entire universe. Could one not turn from a starry night to find in this face the same law in bloom, the same grandeur, depth, inconceivableness?" The title is an editorial addition.

91 "Turning." *Kassner:* Rudolf Kassner (1873–1959), Austrian writer and cultural philosopher, and Rilke's close friend (the eighth *Duino Elegy* is dedicated to him). The epigraph is one of Kassner's "Sayings of the Yogi" (1911), altered by Rilke's strong misremembering of it. Its actual wording is: "He who wants to proceed from inner intensity [*Innigkeit*] to greatness must sacrifice himself."

101 "To Hölderlin." *Hölderlin:* Johann Christian Friedrich Hölderlin (1770–1843), perhaps the greatest German Romantic poet. Rilke read his odes passionately during the summer of 1914.

115 "The Words of the Lord to John on Patmos." Rilke sent the first half of this poem (up through the line "stripping-bare awaits us at the end"), along with a copy of Dürer's *Apocalypse*, to his wife, Clara, as a birthday gift on November 21, 1915. The title is an editorial addition.

133 "The Doll. *Temptation!*" From drafts of a much longer uncompleted elegy on childhood and growing up.

141 " . . . When will, when will, when will it be enough." In a selection of unpublished poems Rilke copied out for Katharina Kippenberg in June 1926, this poem bears the dedication "from M's belongings," along with the postscript "Written on the evening before the Orpheus sonnets."

143 "Antistrophes." Rilke originally conceived this poem as the fifth of the *Duino Elegies*; he replaced it with the "Saltimbanques," the last of the *Elegies* to be composed. (It was written on November 14, five days after "Antistrophes" was completed.)

149 "My shy moonshadow." Compare the ponderous imagery of sphinx and moonscape in the tenth and last *Duino Elegy*, completed on February 11.

153 "Odette R. . . ." Inscribed in *The Notebooks of Malte Laurids Brigge* for Margarethe Masson-Ruffy, in memory of her sister Odette Ruffy, a painter who died young.

157 "Lachrymatory." The second of a two-poem sequence titled "Two Poems" and dedicated to "E.S.," Elisabeth Gundolf-Salomon.

161 "Heart's swing." First draft of a poem inscribed in the *Duino Elegies* for Baladine Klossowska ("Merline"). The inscribed version bears the heading "*Dedication to M. . . . /* Written on the 6th and 8th of November 23 (as beginning of a new winter's work at Muzot)," and follows the draft up to line 18, where it diverges significantly:

> *Or dare I say: quarters? And factor in, since it refuses,*
> *that other half-circle, the one that repels the swing?*
> *It's not my figment, the mere reflection of my earthbound*
> *swinging. This isn't guesswork. One day it shall*
> *be new. But from endpoint to endpoint*
> *of my most reckless swing I already make it fully mine:*
> *overflowings from me stream there and fill it out,*
> *almost tauten it. And my leave-taking,*
> *when the propelling force breaks off from it,*
> *makes it feel to me all the more near.*

167 "For Max Picard." Inscribed in the *Duino Elegies*.

171 "For Hans Carossa." Inscribed in the *Duino Elegies*.

193 "Unsteady scales of life." The fifth of a nine-poem sequence titled "Jottings in the Churchyard at Ragaz."

215 "O bright gleam of a shy mirror image!" The third of a three-poem sequence titled "Three Poems from the Thematic Material [*Umkreis*]: Reflections."

225 "Rose, O pure contradiction." Epitaph composed by Rilke and included in his last will and testament. It is inscribed on his tombstone in the churchyard at Raron, Switzerland.

239 "Brother body is poor." Inscribed by Rilke in the *Book of Images* for his fellow patient Madame Verrijn-Stuart and her husband.

243 "Elegy." *Marina Tsvetayeva* (1892–1941): one of the great modern Russian poets. Without ever meeting, she and Rilke carried on a passionate correspondence during the spring and summer of 1926. Her long poem "Novogodnee," written in early January 1927, addresses Rilke with wild directness, as if in a refusal to grieve. l. 18, *Kom Ombo:* probably a stop on Rilke's trip to Egypt in 1911. What he "saw" there remains obscure, as does the elliptical formulation of a renunciation or "self-withholding" in the poem's next line. Something of what Rilke has in mind may be illuminated by two extraneous passages from his writing. The first is from one of the poems—it concerns

Karnak and the ancient Egyptian friezes—in his cycle *From the Remains of Count C.W.* (November 1920):

> . . . *the god-king, like a suckling child, peaceably*
>
> *receives and smiles. His sacredness*
> *is never short of breath. He takes and takes,*
> *and yet such alleviation reigns in him*
> *that often the princess only clasps*
>
> *the papyrus-flower, instead of breaking it.*—

The second is from a letter to Katharina Kippenberg of May 28, 1924:

> *[Instead of picking flowers from my garden and sending them to you for your birthday on a journey they could never survive,] I will offer them in the manner of the sacrificers on the Egyptian reliefs, who dedicated and presented their flowers to the gods not by picking them, but by holding their hands for a time quietly and intently around the living, growing stems.*

251 "Come, you last thing." The last four lines are canceled in the pocket-book.

Index of Titles and First Lines in German

Aber versuchtest du dies: Hand in der Hand mir zu sein, 232

Ach, da wir Hülfe von Menschen erharrten: stiegen, 18

Ach entzögen wir uns Zählern und Stundenschlägern, 246

Ach, im Wind gelöst, 196

Ach, nicht getrennt sein, 218

Ach wehe, meine Mutter reißt mich ein, 108

Also, das tat not für den und den, 36

Andere fassen den Wein, andere fassen die Öle, 156

An der sonngewohnten Straße, in dem, 188

AN DIE MUSIK, 128

AN HÖLDERLIN, 100

ANKUNFT, 248

AN LOU ANDREAS-SALOMÉ, 12

Auch noch Verlieren ist *unser;* und selbst das Vergessen, 170

AUFERWECKUNG DES LAZARUS, 36

Aufgedeckter das Land: auf allen Wegen ist Heimkehr, 210

Aus dieser Wolke, siehe: die den Stern, 30

Ausgesetzt auf den Bergen des Herzens. Siehe, wie klein dort, 104

Bestürz mich, Musik, mit rhythmischem Zürnen, 70

Bruder Körper ist arm . . . : da heißt es, reich sein für ihn, 238

CHRISTI HÖLLENFAHRT, 64

Da dich das geflügelte Entzücken, 176

Daß wir nichts verlieren, daß auch die, 168

Da stehen wir mit Spiegeln, 166

Da steht der Tod, ein bläulicher Absud, 112

Da wird der Hirsch zum Erdteil. Hebt und trägt, 122

Dich aufdenkend wird mein Wesen erglühter, 68

Die Puppe. *Versuchung,* 132

Dies also: dies geht von mir aus und löst, 60

Dies überstanden haben: auch das Glück, 134

Die Vogelrufe fangen an zu rühmen, 236

Du im Voraus, 86

Durch den sich Vögel werfen, ist nicht der, 190

Endlich verlitten, entging sein Wesen dem schrecklichen, 64

Eine Furche in meinem Hirn, 198

Einmal nahm ich zwischen mein Hände, 80

ELEGIE, 242

Er ruft es an. Es schrickt zusamm und steht, 172

Erst eine Kindheit, grenzenlos und ohne, 154
Fast wie am Jüngsten Tag die Toten sich reißen, 98
Flugsand der Stunden. Leise fortwährende Schwindung, 180
Früher, wie oft, blieben wir, Stern in Stern, 234
FÜR HANS CAROSSA, 170
FÜR MAX PICARD, 166
GEGEN-STROPHEN, 142
GEIST ARIEL, DER, 40
GONG [I], 226
GONG [II], 230
Gott läßt sich nicht wie leichter Morgen leben, 130
Gott oder Göttin des Katzenschlafs, 228
Graue Liebesschlangen hab ich aus deinen, 124
GROSSE NACHT, DIE, 82
HAND, DIE, 136
HANDINNERES, 200
Härte schwand. Auf einmal legt sich Schonung, 178
Hebend die Blicke vom Buch, von den nahen zählbaren Zeilen, 84
HERBST, 212
Hinter den schuld-losen Bäumen, 72
Ich hielt mich überoffen, ich vergaß, 12
Ich Wissender: oh der ich eingeweiht, 26
IDOL, 228
IMAGINÄRER LEBENSLAUF, 154
Immer wieder, ob wir der Liebe Landschaft auch kennen, 106
In einer Rose steht dein Bett, Geliebte. Dich selber, 248
Innres der Hand. Sohle, die nicht mehr geht, 200
Irgendwo blüht die Blume des Abschieds und streut, 208
IRRLICHTER, 174
Jetzt wär es Zeit, daß Götter träten aus, 222
JUDITH'S RÜCKKEHR, 10
Keiner, der finstere nur gefallene Engel, 110
KLAGE, 94
Klang, nichtmehr mit Gehör, 226
Komm du, du letzter, den ich anerkenne, 250
Komm wann du sollst. Dies alles wird durch mich, 22
Königsherz. Kern eines hohen, 206
KOPF AMENOPHIS IV. IN BERLIN, 74
Kreuzweg des Leibes. Und sind doch die himmlischen Straßen, 120
Lange errang ers im Anschaun, 90
Lange mußt du leiden, kennend nicht was, 50
MAGIER, DER, 172
Man hat ihn einmal irgendwo befreit, 40

›MAN MUSS STERBEN WEIL MAN SIE KENNT‹, 96

›Man muß sterben weil man sie kennt.‹ Sterben, 96

MAUSOLEUM, 206

Mein scheuer Mondschatten spräche gern, 148

Mitte, wie du aus allen, 204

MONDNACHT, 8

Musik: Atem der Statuen. Vielleicht, 128

Nacht. Oh du in Tiefe gelöstes, 202

NARZISS [I], 58

NARZISS [II], 60

Narziss verging. Von seiner Schönheit hob, 58

Nicht mehr für Ohren . . . : Klang, 230

Nun wachen wir mit den Erinnerungen, 66

Nur zu Verlierern spricht das Verwandelte. Alle, 126

ODETTE R. . . . , 152

O die Kurven meiner Sehnsucht durch das Weltall, 20

O die Verluste ins All, Marina, die stürzenden Sterne, 242

Oft anstaunt ich dich, stand an gestern begonnenem Fenster, 82

Oh, daß ihr hier, Frauen, einhergeht, 142

Oh hoher Baum des Schauns, der sich entlaubt, 212

O schöner Glanz des scheuen Spiegelbilds, 214

Perlen entrollen. Weh, riß eine der Schnüre, 16

Rose, oh reiner Widerspruch, Lust, 224

Sag weißt du Liebesnächte? Treiben nicht, 4

Scharfer Burgbruch, alter Unterkiefer, 6

Schaukel des Herzens. O sichere, an welchem unsichtbaren, 160

Schläfer, schwarz ist das Naß noch an meinen Füßen, ungenau, 10

Schon ist mein Blick am Hügel, dem besonnten, 182

SCHWERKRAFT, 204

Siehe das leichte Insekt, wie es spielt, nie entriet es, 88

Siehe: (denn kein Baum soll dich zerstreuen), 114

Siehe die kleine Meise, 136

Sieh, wie unsre Schalen sich durchdringen, 150

So angestrengt wider die starke Nacht, 44

Solang du Selbstgeworfnes fängst, ist alles, 138

SPANISCHE TRILOGIE, DIE, 30

SPAZIERGANG, 182

Spiele die Tode, die einzelnen, rasch und du wirst sie erkennen, 164

TOD, DER, 112

TOD MOSES, DER, 110

Tränen, die innigsten, *steigen*, 152

TRÄNENKRÜGLEIN, 156

Tränen, Tränen, die aus mir brechen, 78

Überfließende Himmel verschwendeter Sterne, 56
Unaufhaltsam, ich will die Bahn vollenden, 220
Unendlich staun ich euch an, ihr Seligen, euer Benehmen, 28
Unstete Waage des Lebens, 192
Unwissend vor dem Himmel meines Lebens, 54
VASEN-BILD, 150
VERGÄNGLICHKEIT, 180
Vergiß, vergiß und laß uns jetzt nur dies, 2
Verweilung, auch am Vertrautesten nicht, 100
VOLLMACHT, 246
Von nahendem Regen fast zärtlich verdunkelter Garten, 240
VORFRÜHLING, 178
. . . Wann wird, wann wird, wann wird es genügen, 140
Weg in den Garten, tief wie ein langes Getränke, 8
Weißt du nicht, wird der Rotdorn bald, 52
Weißt du noch: fallende Sterne, die, 184
Welt war in dem Antlitz der Geliebten, 194
Wem willst du klagen, Herz? Immer gemiedener, 94
WENDUNG, 90
. . . Wenn aus des Kaufmanns Hand, 216
Wie das Gestirn, der Mond, erhaben, voll Anlaß, 76
Wie junge Wiesen, blumig, einen Abhang, 74
Wie steht er da vor den Verdunkelungen, 186
WILDER ROSENBUSCH, 186
Wir haben einen alten Verkehr, 174
Wir, in den ringenden Nächten, 146
Wir sind nur Mund. Wer singt das ferne Herz, 158
Wir wissen nicht, was wir verbringen: siehe, 48
WORTE DES HERRN AN JOHANNES AUF PATMOS, DIE, 114

Index of Titles and First Lines in English

A furrow in my brain, 199
Again and again, even though we know love's landscape, 107
Ah, adrift in the air, 197
Ah, as we prayed for human help: angels soundlessly, 19
Ah, could we escape counters and strikers of hours, 247
Ah misery, my mother tears me down, 109
Ah, not to be cut off, 219
Ah, women, that you are here on earth, that you, 143
Almost as on the last day the dead will tear themselves, 99
Already my gaze is on the hill, that sunlit one, 183
Always I marvel at you, you blessed ones,—at your demeanor, 29
And here we have Death, a bluish distillate, 113
And so we stand with mirrors, 167
And this: this escapes from me and dissolves, 61
ANTISTROPHES, 143
ARRIVAL, 249
As long as you catch self-thrown things, 139
As once the winged energy of delight, 177
Assault me, music, with rhythmic fury, 71
As young meadows, flowerfilled, through, 75
AUTUMN, 213
Behind the innocent trees, 73
Behold: (for no tree shall distract you), 115
Brother body is poor . . . : then we'll have to be rich for him, 239
But if you'd try this: to be hand in my hand, 233
By the sun-accustomed street, in the, 189
Center, how you from all things living, 205
CHRIST'S DESCENT INTO HELL, 65
Come when you should. All this will have been, 23
Come, you last thing, which I acknowledge, 251
DEATH, 113
DEATH OF MOSES, THE, 111
Do you still remember: falling stars, how, 185
Driftsand of hours. Quietly continuous fading, 181
Earlier, how often, we'd remain, star in star, 235
EARLY SPRING, 179
ELEGY, 243
Finally suffered-out, his being exited the terrible, 65

First a childhood, boundless and without, 155

Forget, forget, and let us live now, 3

FOR HANS CAROSSA, 171

FOR MAX PICARD, 167

From this cloud—look: that so wildly covers, 31

FULL POWER, 247

Garden, by approaching rains almost tenderly darkened, 241

God or goddess of the sleep of cats, 229

God won't be lived like some light morning, 131

GONG [I], 227

GONG [II], 231

GRAVITY, 205

Gray love-snakes I have startled, 125

GREAT NIGHT, THE, 83

HAND, THE, 137

Hand's secret self. Sole, that has ceased to walk, 201

Harshness disappeared. Suddenly caring spreads itself, 179

HEAD OF AMENOPHIS IV IN BERLIN, 75

Heart's swing. O so securely fastened, 161

He calls it up. It startles into outline, 173

He had long won it through gazing, 91

How it stands out against the darkenings, 187

IDOL, 229

I held myself too open, I forgot, 13

I, knower: possessing the secrets, 27

IMAGINARY CAREER, 155

Imagining you my being burns more brightly, 69

Inside a rose your bed stands, beloved. You yourself, 249

JUDITH'S RETURN, 11

King's heart. Core of a high, 207

LACHRYMATORY, 157

LAMENT, 95

Lingering, even among what's most intimate, 101

Long you must suffer, knowing not what, 51

Looking up from my book, from the close countable lines, 85

Losing also is ours; and even forgetting, 171

MAGICIAN, THE, 173

MAUSOLEUM, 207

MOONLIT NIGHT, 9

More unconcealed the land. On every road returnings, 211

Music: breathing of statues. Perhaps, 129

My shy moonshadow would like to speak, 149

NARCISSUS [I], 59

NARCISSUS [II], 61

Narcissus vanished. His beauty gave off, 59

Night. Oh you face against my face, 203

No longer for ears . . . : sound, 231

None of them, only the dark, fallen angel, 111

Now it is time that gods stepped out, 223

Now the stag becomes part of earth. Lifts and holds, 123

Now we wake up with our memory, 67

O bright gleam of a shy mirror image, 215

ODETTE R. . . . , 153

Often I stared at you, stood at the window begun yesterday, 83

Oh gazing's tall tree, shedding leaf on leaf, 213

Once I took your face into, 81

Once long ago somewhere you freed him, 41

"ONE MUST DIE BECAUSE ONE HAS KNOWN THEM," 97

"One must die because one has known them." Die, 97

On the mountains of the heart cast out to die. Look, how small there, 105

O the curves of my longing through the cosmos, 21

O the losses into the All, Marina, the falling stars, 243

Others carry the wine, others carry the oil, 157

Overflowing heavens of squandered stars, 57

PALM OF THE HAND, 201

Path in the garden, deep as a long drink, 9

Pearls roll away. Ah, one of the strings broke, 17

Play the deaths swiftly through, the single ones, and you will see, 165

RAISING OF LAZARUS, THE, 37

Rose, O pure contradiction, delight, 225

See how our cups penetrate each other, 151

See the carefree insect, how it plays, its whole world, 89

See the little titmouse, 137

Sharp castle-break, ancient underjaw, 7

Sleepers, the damp on my feet is still black, indistinct, 11

Somewhere the flower of farewell blooms and scatters, 209

Sound, no longer measurable, 227

SPANISH TRILOGY, THE, 31

SPIRIT ARIEL, THE, 41

Straining so hard against the strength of night, 45

Tears, tears that break out of me, 79

Tears, those most intensely felt, *rise*, 153

That we lose nothing, that even those, 169

The birdcalls begin their praise, 237

The body's crossroads: and yet the heavenly streets, 121

The Doll. *Temptation*, 133

The hawthorn there: who would guess, 53

The transformed speaks only to relinquishers. All, 127

The way that bright planet, the moon, exalted, full of purpose, 77

To have come through it: to have joyfully, 135

TO HÖLDERLIN, 101

TO LOU ANDREAS-SALOMÉ, 13

TO MUSIC, 129

To whom, heart, would you lament? Ever more avoided, 95

TRANSIENCE, 181

TURNING, 91

Undeterrable, I'll complete this course, 221

Unknowing before the heavens of my life, 55

Unsteady scales of life, 193

VASE PAINTING, 151

WALK, A, 183

We don't know what we spend, 49

We have an old obscure connection, 175

We, in the grappling nights, 147

We're only mouth. Who sings the distant heart, 159

What birds plunge through is not that intimate space, 191

. . . When from the merchant's hand, 217

. . . When will, when will, when will it be enough, 141

WILD ROSEBUSH, 187

WILL-O'-THE-WISPS, 175

WORDS OF THE LORD TO JOHN ON PATMOS, THE, 115

World was in the face of the beloved, 195

Yes, it was necessary for this common sort, 37

You don't know nights of love? Don't, 5

You the beloved, 87